The NEW LIFE COOK- BOOK

Based on the health and nutritional
philosophy of the Edgar Cayce readings

THE NEW LIFE COOK-BOOK

Based on the health and nutritional philosophy of the Edgar Cayce readings

by
MARCELINE A. NEWTON

Introduction by Hugh Lynn Cayce

THE
DONNING COMPANY
PUBLISHERS
NORFOLK/VIRGINIA BEACH

First printing June 1976
Second printing August 1977
Third printing June 1978
Fourth printing October 1980
Fifth printing December 1982
Sixth printing August 1989

Library of Congress Cataloging in Publication Data:
Newton, Marceline A.   1940-
The new life cook book.
Bibliography: p.
1. Cookery (Natural foods) I. Cayce, Edgar, 1877-
1945. II. Title.
TX741.N48   641.5'636   76-15963
ISBN 0-915442-13-2

Printed in the United States of America

Contents

Introduction

Nine thousand Edgar Cayce health readings contain suggestions about diet. One of the best ways that we have found to get people thinking about diet is to actually provide them with suggestions for tasty good food in the right combinations. Here is our latest effort, in cooperation with Marcie Newton, who handles the kitchen at the Marshalls Hotel, the A.R.E. conference headquarters at Virginia Beach, Virginia. She and her staff have served good meals to literally thousands of persons who come for the regular twenty weeks of A.R.E. Conferences and to members and friends who have stopped to visit our Library/Conference Center. This number is growing, and on every hand we have been hearing conferees asking again and again: How do you make this? Give me the recipe for this! Here they are.

Marcie has fifteen years nutritional experience. (The way she says it is, "I love to cook!") With the help of the young people in the A.R.E. Work-Study Program, she has put together selections from the Edgar Cayce readings on which the basic plan for the meals at the Marshalls is developed. Here, in an easily readable form, are suggestions and recipes that will enable anyone to follow the overall dietary plan as suggested by the Edgar Cayce health readings. This is a usable, practical guide. It may indeed make a new person out of you as you start using it every day.

Hugh Lynn Cayce

Foreword

The Marshalls Hotel in Virginia Beach is affiliated with the Association for Research and Enlightenment, and has provided accommodations for visitors to the Foundation for many years. One day, in the hotel dining room, two conferees came up to me. They asked me about the food they had just eaten. I smiled, and as I can recollect, told them it was eggplant parmigiana. As I began to explain the recipe, a vibration came over me to tell all to the beautiful people who had complimented me on the foods they had eaten over the years at the Marshalls, where I had been cook, nutritionist, and food manager for eight years.

With this thought in mind I spoke to Hugh Lynn Cayce. I was challenged and surprised by his answer: "Marcie, write a book." I called a meeting of my work-study group, because if this were to come about, I would need their help. Their faces were a ray of God's sunshine; this I will never forget. I often forget to call them by name because we are a family away from home, trying to serve the people from all over the world who come to the A.R.E. for research, lectures, and conferences.

To them, my Marshalls children, whom I love so deeply, go my greatest thanks for helping me to prepare this book. There is no mystique here. We simply enjoy serving people and we love good food. Everybody loves to eat!

When I cook, I care about the look, taste, and smell of the food. I always add love and lots of good vibration to the ingredients. I attempt to turn the daily routine of cooking for three hundred and fifty people into a beautiful seven-day happening. When you have good food, and good vibrations from people with whom you're eating, it's the kind of happening that turns me on.

So now, with all my love and help from the work-study group, here are my tried and tested recipes for the wonderful people who have dined at the Marshalls and who would like to apply Edgar Cayce's philosophy of diet in their own lives—and for those who seek to eat food which is not only healthy, but delicious. After all, Edgar Cayce said many times that we are what we eat, and that's what I believe, too.

Marceline A. Newton
Virginia Beach, March 1976

Definition of Terms

Bake: Cook by dry heat, usually in the oven; for meats, it is called roasting.

Barbecue: Roast meat slowly on a spit over coals or in the oven, basting frequently with a highly seasoned sauce.

Baste: Moisten foods during cooking with pan drippings, water, or special sauce to prevent drying or to add flavor.

Beat: Make mixture smooth by using a wire whip or stirring with a spoon or electric mixer.

Blanch: Pour boiling water over food to loosen skin, remove color, or set color.

Blend: Mix two or more ingredients until smooth and uniform.

Boil: Cook in liquid in which bubbles rise constantly to the surface and break.

Braise: Brown in a small amount of hot fat, then add a small amount of liquid and cook slowly in a tightly covered utensil on top of range or in oven.

Bread: Coat with bread crumbs or mixture of beaten egg and milk, then crumbs.

Broil: Cook by direct heat, usually in broiler or over coals.

Candy: Cook in sugar or syrup when applied to sweet potatoes and carrots. For fruit, fruit peel, or ginger, to cook in heavy syrup until plump and transparent.

Caramelize: Melt sugar slowly over low heat until it becomes brown in color.

Chop: Cut in pieces with knife, chopper, or scissors.

Cream: Beat or rub with spoon or electric mixer until mixture is soft and fluffy.

Cut in: Mix shortening with dry ingredients, using pastry blender, knife, or fork.

Dice: Cut food in small cubes of uniform size.

Dissolve: Cause a dry substance to pass into solution in a liquid.

Dredge: Sprinkle or coat with flour or other fine substance.

Flake: Break lightly into small pieces.

Fold in: Add new ingredients to a mixture that's beaten until light by cutting down through mixture with spoon, wire whip, or fork, then going across bottom of bowl, up and over, close to the surface.

Fricassee: Cook by braising; usually applied to fowl or rabbit.

Fry: Cook in a hot fat; to cook in a fat is called pan-frying or sautéing; to cook in a one- to two-inch layer of hot fat is called shallow-fat frying; to cook in a deep layer of hot fat is called deep-fat frying.

Glaze: Coat with a thin or slightly thickened sugar syrup cooked to crack stage, or to cover with a thin icing.

Grate: Rub on a grater that separates the food in various sizes or bits or shreds.

Knead: Work and press dough with the palms of the hands.

Marinate: Allow a food to stand in a liquid.

Mince: Cut or chop food into extremely small pieces.

Mix: Combine ingredients, usually by stirring.

Pan-broil: Cook uncovered in a hot fry pan, pouring off fat as it accumulates.

Pan-fry: Cook in a small amount of fat.

Pasteurize: Preserve food by heating sufficiently to destroy bacteria, generally applied to milk and fruit juices.

Pit: Remove seed or pit.

Poach: Cook in a hot liquid, being careful that food holds shape.

Roast: Cook by dry heat, usually in oven.

Sauté: Cook in small amount of hot fat.

Scald: Bring to a temperature just below the boiling point.

Scallop: Bake a food, usually in a casserole with sauce or other liquid; crumbs often are sprinkled over the surface.

Score: Cut narrow grooves or gashes partway through the outer surface of food.

Sear: Brown the surface of meat quickly over high heat.

Shred: Cut food into slivers or slender pieces, using a knife or shredder.

Sift: Put one or more dry ingredients through a sieve or sifter.

Simmer: Cook slowly in liquid over low heat, at a temperature of about 180 degrees.

Steam: Cook in steam in a pressure cooker, deep-well cooker, double boiler, or a steamer made by fitting a rack in a kettle with a tight cover, using a small amount of boiling water and adding more water during the steaming process if necessary.

Steep: Allow food to stand in hot liquid to extract flavor and color.

Sterilize: Destroy micro-organisms by boiling, dry heat, or steam.

Stew: Simmer slowly in a small amount of liquid for a long time.

Stir: Mix ingredients with a circular motion until well blended.

Truss: Tie fowl or other meat with metal or wooden pins (skewers) to hold its shape during cooking.

Whip: Beat rapidly with mixer, hand beater, or wire whisk so air is incorporated and volume is increased.

My Favorite Tips

To ripen fruit more quickly, bury it in your meal bin.

To save washing an extra cup, measure dry ingredients first, place ingredients on a sheet of wax paper, then use the same cup for liquids.

To test eggs for freshness, place them in a deep bowl of cold water. Fresh eggs will sink to the bottom of the bowl.

Cheeses that have become hard and dry after long storage in the refrigerator may be cut into small pieces and grated in a blender. Store in a plastic bag for use in casserole toppings, in sauces, etc.

To save time making herbal or iced tea, fill a quart container with cold water and add tea. Place in refrigerator for several hours or until tea is the desired strength. Tea will be clear with a sparkling flavor.

To keep hands from smelling "fishy" after handling raw fish, chill them in cold water before you touch fish.

Rubbing the hands with a slice of lemon keeps off offensive odors.

For grating cheese without a mess on the grater, put cheese in the freezer one half-hour prior to grating.

To peel boiled eggs faster, pour hot water off at once and shake the pan five or six times. Then pour cold water over the eggs. They practically slide out of the shell.

Garlic oil can be made quickly and will last for ages if you place peeled garlic buds in a jar and cover with your favorite oil. I use peanut or soy oil. Let stand tightly covered in refrigerator. Use in salads, on meat, as needed.

To plant garlic, put an unpeeled bud of garlic root, wide end down, in a glass with a bit of water. Leave for three days. Plant in a small pot of soil (empty condiment shakers are very good for this). The garlic grows about a foot high. When needed, just snip off like you would chives.

When making dressings for your holiday turkey, always make three times as much as you need, and freeze the unused dressing in divided portions. Pop out as needed. It's a real time saver and your family will love it.

For instant peanut butter, put fresh roasted peanuts in the blender and blend until creamy or chunky. Honey may be added if you desire. This will help prevent tearing the bread slices, plus the kids will love it.

If you have whipping cream left over, place it in your mixer and beat until you have a delicious natural piece of fresh butter. I use this when the work-study group over-whips the whipping cream.

Rice pudding made from leftover eggnog is great; just use the eggnog instead of milk.

To clean a waffle iron, use a small stiff brush.

To extract juice from a lemon when a small amount is needed, puncture the skin with a fork and squeeze gently.

To avoid wrinkled skins on baked apples, slit the apples at the bottom in a thin round circle.

To prevent dried fruits from clogging up the food blender, add a few drops of lemon juice just before grinding.

Cut fresh baked bread with a hot knife for better slices.

To keep sweet potatoes and apples from turning black, place them in salted cold water at once after peeling.

To keep fresh parsley, mint, and watercress: wash, shake off excess water, put in a jar, cover tightly, and refrigerate.

To remove odors from jars, shake dry mustard and water into them (presto).

Abbreviations

C. = cup
doz. = dozen
gal. = gallon
lg. = large
oz. = ounce
pkg. = package
pt. = pint
lb. = pound
qt. = quart
sm. = small
tbsp. = tablespoon
tsp. = teaspoon

The Marshalls Kitchen

From the readings of Edgar Cayce, the famous psychic, No. 5399:
"It is not so important what goes in the mouth, but what comes out."

In keeping with Cayce's holistic approach to living, meals prepared at the Marshalls are intended to nourish our body, mind, and soul. Whole grains, short-cooked fresh vegetables, bean sprouts, herb teas, yogurt, honey, mineral water—these foods are not typically found in hotel restaurants and perhaps are not yet established in your regular diet. Relax—we're all learning here! Let us share with you the things we find beneficial to a temple of the living God. What you'll be eating is the best that earth and man can offer with love.

Edgar Cayce recommends the diet to be about eighty percent alkaline ash and about twenty percent acid ash foods, or in the proportion of four vegetables and two fruits to one protein and one starch. This is not to be kept rigidly, but according to the body's needs—when under stress or nervous anxiety, the body requires more fruits and vegetables. Of the vegetable types, one below ground to two above ground and one leafy to one pod variety are suggested proportions. Citrus fruits are not to be combined with grains, for this causes over-acidity; this applies also to a coffee-milk combination, or heavy starch-protein. Sweet or dried fruits are better combined with starches than with proteins. See chapter four of *Edgar Cayce on Diet and Health* for more information on acid-alkaline foods.

Those of you already attuned to natural foods know that small portions more than adequately nourish and satisfy; the need for quantity is a result of devitalized processed foods. All are most welcome to additional servings, but do avoid unnecessary waste. Avoiding waste is what "eating low on the food chain" is all about. It is a waste of time, money, energy, health, and ecology to produce and consume foodstuffs not only robbed of their nutritional elements, but filled with chemicals and additives that are drosses to the system. That which is sown, prepared, and consumed with love is of the one vibration. And isn't love what it's all about?

So it's really not food I am talking about at all, but vibration: the food is a manifested idea.

"Natural" foods are not devitalized: they contain the essential life forces; they are whole; they have grown at their own pace. I want you to grow at your natural pace as well. There isn't anyone who takes easily to change of habit, but the gradual growth—the building step by step—is the firm foundation.

Our serving of natural foods is not meant as a "this-is-the-way" precept or as a denial of your freedom of choice, but simply as an introduction to the alternative. I don't want to harness you with strange foods; it's all quite as American as apple pie—the kind your grandmother used to bake: fresh apples from the orchard and flour ground at the local mill.

Thus it will not matter so much what is eaten or where or when, but just knowing it is consistent with what is desired to be accomplished through the body—that does matter.

The health, security, and pleasure of the Marshalls clientele depend on my skill in planning meals, so I treat my job with the respect that is due it. I want to take pride in doing an outstanding job of cooking. Above all I want happiness from work itself.

Grains: Ours come from organic sources, grown with patience and respect for the soil, with no poisonous sprays or chemical hurry-uppers. The flours are stone ground and unfumigated, meaning they are not heated and "purified" of their nutritional elements in the process of milling. The whole grain berry consists of a bran (a covering), a germ (the seed of new life, or the life force), and an endosperm (food for the germ). The bran and the germ contain vitamins, minerals, and amino acids (protein fibers). The endosperm by itself has little nutritive value for us (this is the bulk content of white rice, white bread); however, converted naturally by the germ into high concentrate protein (that's what's good about bean sprouts and fertilized eggs), or when eaten together with the bran and germ, the endosperm is more than glutenous starch; it seems to act much the same as natural gelatin in that it facilitates digestion. Whole grains are also natural laxatives; taken daily they foster an assimilations-eliminations balance essential to the body's well-being. When combined with compatible protein sources such as legumes, nuts, and seeds, grains form easily assimilated complete proteins, for the amino acids typically lacking in one food are found complemented in another. Some of the grains you'll be eating: *bulgur*, a parboiled cracked wheat used as a staple in the Near East, has a soft texture and nutty flavor; *wheat berries*, the whole grain from whence our basic flours come, is chewy textured and mild flavored; the bland tasting *millet*, a rarity in the grain world because it has an alkaline ash, is quite high in protein and is a grass staple in China. *Brown rice* is, of course, the whole rice berry, high in nutrients and easily digestible.

Legumes: Acid ash dried beans, peas, and lentils are good protein sources that combine well with grains. The *soybean* is the most nutritionally complete of the beans, has an alkaline ash, and a scant starch content. Derivatives of soy are used frequently as nutritional boosters: *miso* (soybean puree), *tamari* (natural soy sauce), *lecithin* (a phosphates concentrate that helps dissolve fats), *soya flour, soya grits, soya milk, tofu* (soy cheese), and *soy oil*—you can be sure the versatile soy is daily utilized here. *Soya-egg noodles*, having an alkaline base, take the edge off an ill-advised protein-starch combination such as macaroni and cheese, or the equally heavy citrus-starch combination of spaghetti with tomatoes.

Vegetables (alkaline ash): Leafy greens and tubers grow well in Virginia, and we have a local organic source for these. Other fresh vegetables are shipped commercially, and "fresh frozen" are served for variety. (Plum tomatoes and whole baby beets are the only canned vegetables we stock.) Vegetables are either steamed, short-cooked, or baked and served with their jackets for greatest vitamin content. Our soups are homemade, seasoned with herbs and natural nutritional boosters. Also, no leftovers are served without added nutrients. Vegetables, raw or short-cooked, are highly recommended in the Cayce readings as blood purifiers rich in vitamins and minerals. We serve plenty of leafy green salads with our own high-protein dressings. Fresh carrot or orange juice can be had upon request.

Fruits (alkaline ash): We've no organic sources for fresh fruits as yet, but the dried fruits—prune, apricot, date, raisin, fig—are additive-free and naturally processed. We keep fewer and fewer canned fruits on hand, except those packed in water. Natural fruit sugars carry trace elements and enzymes necessary for conversion to blood sugar. Taking a raw fruit at mid-morning is beneficial. Citrus should not be taken with grain, as this causes over-acidity in the system. Raw apple should not be combined with anything.

Dairy Products: Cayce classified egg yolk, milk, and milk products as alkaline ash foods. Instant powdered skim milk is used in our cooking, as milk is more easily digested and higher in protein when defatted.

Meats, Fish, and Poultry (acid ash): Though good sources of protein, commercially processed animal foods are injected with tenderizers, preservatives, and sugar. Unfortunately we have not located a reasonable organic source for these products. We do rely heavily upon poultry, fish, lamb, and organ meats, which Cayce considered more beneficial than beef or pork. The chickens, and sometimes the fish, we obtain fresh and cut into portions ourselves.

Nuts and Seeds: High protein sources with an acid ash, almonds, sunflower, and sesame seeds contain the life force (the germ) and essential fatty acids. Nut butters and nut meal are also beneficial.

Hi-Pro Salad Dressings: Our own dressings are prepared with a base of egg yolk, olive oil, apple cider vinegar, fresh lemon juice, sea kelp, bleu cheese, and sour cream, and are enhanced with the subtle flavoring of ground seed or nut meats and various herbs.

Marshalls Bread: Using stone ground flours, honey, molasses, natural dried yeast, and cold-pressed oils, the staff of life is baked with love.

Mineral Water: Truly a pure food for the body, free of chlorinated chemicals, this water carries natural earth minerals and trace elements.

Sea Kelp: A salt substitute, this powdered sea green contains many trace elements and high potency iodine. Beneficial for glandular regulation and particularly for balance in the thyroid gland, kelp is also of late considered a cancer preventative.

Brewers Yeast: A by-product of the beer brewing industry, this high-quality protein food contains the vitamin B complex, and all the essential minerals and amino acids. Palatable quantities are used as nutritional supplements.

Carob Powder (St. John's Bread): An alkaline chocolate substitute, high in natural sugars and calcium and low in fat and starch, this powder is made from dried carob pods, a fruit also known as locust. It is said St. John ate only honey and locusts in the desert.

Honey and Molasses: Uncooked honey is an alkaline food containing minerals that aid assimilation. Whereas white (cane) sugar robs your cells of their nutrients, honey feeds them. We use scant sugar in our baking and cooking. (Note that brown sugar and "raw" sugar are both white sugar with small percentages of molasses added. The detriment of sugar in the system outweighs the benefit of the molasses. See chapter seven of *Edgar Cayce on Diet and Health* for a detailed sugar story.)

Unsulphured blackstrap molasses is from the third pressing of the cane, and at this stage contains high quantities of minerals and vitamins, even more than honey. It is especially high in potassium and calcium.

Yogurt: High in B vitamins and more easily digested than milk, yogurt hosts a bacterial culture very beneficial to the colon and the process of eliminations. Ours is made with powdered skim milk for a low fat content. To make one quart of yogurt: combine ¾ C. plain yogurt (without gelatin) or yogurt culture with 1 qt. skim milk or reconstituted non-fat dry milk. Place in yogurt maker or glass container. Leave overnight in a closed oven; if gas, leave pilot light burning; if electric, preheat to 250° then turn off heat.

Bean Sprouts: In this stage of growth the germ, or life force, of the seed converts the endosperm into high concentrate protein. Frequently served here are mung, alfalfa, lentil, and wheat berry sprouts.

Natural Gelatin: Derived from the cow hoof, gelatin is a great aid to protein digestion. Cayce suggested taking it daily. We use natural fruits and honey in the gelatin desserts, and vegetables and juices in the aspics.

Cold-Pressed Oils: These oils are extracted by steam pressure rather than petroleum-based solvents, and contain no chemical additives. Edible oils provide the essential fatty acids which *decrease* your body's cholesterol production.

Clarified Butter (Ghee): Ghee is the sweet aromatic liquid which remains when the animal fats are removed by heat from the butter. Solidified saturated fats *increase* cholsterol production, and animal fats have been found to be high retainers of pesticide residue and other environmental contaminants.

Baking Powder: Cayce suggested Royal baking powder, but since it cannot easily be found in some areas, you can make your own, eliminating unwanted chemicals, from this recipe: Combine 1 portion of cream of tartar with 3 portions of baking soda.

Herbal Teas: Free of tannin and caffeine, soothing and delicious, most herb teas contain vitamins and minerals and are medicinal—aiding digestion, soothing mucous membranes, purifying the bloodstream, organs, and glands of the body. Herbal teas are wonderful beverages; there are many types to choose from. The most popular ones at the Marshalls are alfalfa, camomile, sassafras, mo's 24, spearmint, peppermint, rosehips, orange peel, peach, red clover, and sundry blends.

You can mix rose hips with almost any of the above. Add a squeeze of lemon and a bit of honey and you have a delicious beverage. And it's so natural. The children will love them in a big way. And guess what? They are harmless.

Mix them with juices such as apple, cranberry, grape, and pineapple, and delight your guests with these punches. Garnish with mint, ice cubes, and orange or lemon slices. Even a floating lily or rose is very festive.

Kitchen Utensils: Edgar Cayce advised against the use of all aluminum utensils because of the softness of the compound mixture. Aluminum can dissolve into food and be ingested. I suggest the use of the following equipment for cooking: stainless steel, cast iron, porcelain-coated cast iron, heat-resistant glass or stoneware casserole dishes, glass or steel pie pans, and soup pots of steel or porcelain.

The following books are used at the Marshalls, and are highly recommended for any basic understanding of beneficial food combinations, acid-alkaline balance, minimum daily requirements, and how to live with our mother earth in a manner most natural and least destructive to both her and ourselves.

Ann, Adrian. *Herbal Tea Book*. Los Angeles: Health Publishing Co., 1959. A basic and easy-going primer; telling how herbs taste and what they do.

Davis, Adelle, *Let's Cook It Right*. New York: Harcourt, Brace, Jovanovich, Inc., 1962. Detailed nutritional advice.

Hunter, Beatrice Trum. *The Natural Foods Cookbook*. New York: Simon and Schuster, 1961. A complete and enjoyable primer and recipe guide.

Lappe, Frances Moore. *Diet for a Small Planet*. New York: Ballantine Books, Inc., 1971. Important research on non-animal protein combinations.

Read, Anne, Carol Ilstrup and Margaret Gammon. *Edgar Cayce on Diet and Health*. New York: Warner Paperback Library, 1969. A guide to the Edgar Cayce readings on nutrition and health.

Appetizers

When friends and family gather, it is always in good taste to serve some appetizing morsels of food. They can be anything from decorative little tea sandwiches, creamy patés, tasty cheese tidbits, hot dips or nut treats to a smorgasbord.

Almond Puffs with Chicken

1 C. whole wheat flour	4 eggs
Dash of salt	1 C. chopped chicken
¾ C. butter	4 tbsp. chopped toasted almonds
1 C. chicken stock	Dash of paprika

Preheat oven to 450°. Do not sift flour; add salt to flour. Combine butter and chicken stock in a medium sauce pan; keep over low heat until butter is melted. Add flour all at once and stir until mixture leaves sides of pan. Remove from heat and beat eggs in one at a time; continue beating until a thick dough is formed. Stir in chicken, almonds, and paprika. Drop by teaspoonfuls on greased cookie sheet. Bake 10 minutes at 450°, reduce heat to 350°, and bake 5 to 10 minutes until golden brown.

Cheese and Yogurt Dip

1 C. cream cheese	1 tbsp. dill seeds
½ C. yogurt	

Beat cream cheese until smooth. Add yogurt and beat until fluffy. Add dill seeds and let sit at room temperature for 10 minutes. This dip is quite nice with wheat thins or melba toast.

Salmon Spread

2 C. canned salmon	Horseradish to taste
½ C. mayonnaise	

Mix together until slightly lumpy. This spread is at its best on cut sourdough or French bread.

Beet Appetizer

Fold baby beets into generous amounts of sour cream. Serve on a lettuce leaf.

Cucumbers at Their Best

Take garden fresh cukes and slice them on a slant. Marinate 1 hour in Italian dressing. Sprinkle with chopped pimiento.

Anchovy Paté

2 eight oz. pkg. cream cheese	½ tsp. mustard
4 walnut size balls of butter	1 tsp. paprika
1 can anchovy fillets, mashed	Garlic
1 sweet onion, grated	

Mix cream cheese and butter well. Add remaining ingredients, except garlic. Serve in a bowl rubbed with garlic; serve with toasted whole wheat squares.

Sesame-Cheese Paste

2 oz. sesame seeds	8 oz. pkg. cream cheese
½ tsp. soy sauce	

Toast sesame seeds lightly in oven. Mix in soy sauce. Pour mixture over block of cream cheese at room temperature. Serve with crackers or toast squares.

Toasted Cheese Squares

⅓ C. Parmesan cheese, grated
¾ C. mayonnaise

½ C. chopped onions
Dash of Worcestershire sauce

Combine all ingredients. Spread on rye squares and toast under broiler for 1 or 2 minutes.

My Best Swiss Fondue

½ lb. butter
1½ C. flour
1½ thirteen oz. cans
    evaporated milk

4 C. Swiss cheese cubes
1 C. white wine

Melt butter in a large saucepan and blend in flour with a wire whisk until smooth. Add evaporated milk, 1 can of water, and cheese. Allow cheese to melt while constantly stirring. Take off heat and stir in your favorite white wine (mine is Liebfraumilch from 1971).

Cheese and Chili Dip

8 oz. cheese spread
    or melted cheese
4 oz. green chili peppers, chopped

Corn chips

Mix cheese spread and chili peppers together until smooth. Serve with corn chips.

Sardine and Cheese Canapés

Mix equal portions of sardines and cream cheese together. Spread the mixture on squares of whole wheat bread. Toast under broiler 2 or 3 minutes.

Brazil Nut Cheese Canapés

½ lb. Monterey Jack cheese, grated
Paprika to taste

Onion juice to taste
Brazil nuts, grated

Mix cheese, paprika, and a little onion juice together. Spread this on whole wheat bread or rye thins, and sprinkle with grated Brazil nuts. An electric blender does a wonderful job of "grating" nuts.

Smoked Salmon Canapés

Spread toasted whole wheat fingers with lemon butter. Place sliced smoked salmon (lox) on toast and serve. You might want to garnish with a few parsley leaves or cayenne.

Stuffed Prunes and Dates

Slit pitted prunes and dates. Stuff with chopped celery, artichoke hearts, or cream cheese. Serve on a platter with wheat thins in the center and stuffed prunes and dates arranged around the edge.

Fresh Fruit Kabob I (Citrus)

2 ripe pineapples
1 pkg. fresh lg. strawberries
1 pkg. wooden skewers

3 fresh mandarin oranges
   or clementines

Cut top and bottom from one pineapple. Peel, core, and cut into inch cubes. Set aside. Cut other pineapple bottom off and place in the middle of a platter. Wash fresh strawberries, leave stem and leaves on, set aside. Peel and section oranges. Place fruit on skewers in this pattern: strawberry with stem at end near fingers, pineapple cube, orange. Stick sharp end of skewer in pineapple in the center of a platter and continue until pineapple and dish are filled. Very festive, and so natural and good.

Fresh Fruit Kabob II (Melon)

1 watermelon	1 pkg. wooden skewers
3 honeydews	1 lg. head Bibb lettuce
3 cantaloupes	

Cut watermelon in half, widthwise, and set one half upside down in the center of a large platter. Place lettuce leaves around edges, covering the entire dish. Peel other half of watermelon and cube in one-inch pieces. Cut honeydew in half, remove seeds, and ball with melon baller. Do the same thing with cantaloupe. Slide fruit on skewer in this pattern: watermelon cube, honeydew ball, watermelon cube, and cantaloupe ball. Stick kabob in first half of watermelon in center of platter. Place any leftover fruit all around the platter on lettuce. This is a wonderful centerpiece.

Anchovy Sticks

1 lg. Bermuda onion, minced	1 tsp. nutmeg
4 tbsp. olive oil	4 tbsp. grated Parmesan cheese
½ C. Swiss cheese, grated	1 loaf whole wheat
3 C. anchovy fillets	bread, unsliced

Sauté onions in olive oil; add Swiss cheese, anchovies, nutmeg, and Parmesan cheese to onion when done. Spread this mixture over bread sliced in four oblong strips. Bake at 400° for 10 minutes. Cut in squares and serve.

Herbal Sticks

This recipe is used on "Wine and Cheese" night at the Marshalls. It's a very special treat. Serve with aged Cheddar cheese.

3 C. all purpose flour	1 tbsp. each: marjoram, thyme,
6 tbsp. Royal baking powder	sweet basil
2 tsp. salt	3 eggs
4 tbsp. raw sugar	2½ C. milk
1½ C. corn meal	1 lb. butter, melted

Sift flour with baking powder, salt, and sugar. Stir in corn meal and herbs.

In another bowl, beat eggs; stir in milk and melted butter. Add dry ingredients and stir just until moist. Spoon into corn stick pans and bake in a hot oven at 400° until golden. Makes approximately 65 sticks.

Ripe Olives Supreme

Drain black olives. Pit them and marinate in Italian dressing with 2 tbsp. curry powder.

Cheese Balls

10 oz. sharp Cheddar cheese, grated	2 tbsp. minced green peppers
2 eight oz. pkg. cream cheese	2 tsp. garlic juice
2 tbsp. minced onion	1 tsp. lemon juice
	Chopped walnuts or pecans

Blend all ingredients together except nuts. Shape into 1 large ball or several small balls. Roll in chopped nuts. Serve with crackers, rye bread, or homemade sesame sticks.

Cheese Puffs

8 oz. cheese spread or melted cheese	¾ C. flour
¼ C. butter	Pitted ripe olives
	Green olives

Mix first 3 ingredients together. Flatten 1 tsp. of the cheese mixture in palm and mold around an olive, rolling into a ball. Place on a cookie sheet in the freezer until firm. Bake at 450° for 8 to 10 minutes.

Marinated Mushrooms

1 tbsp. basil	1 C. vinegar
1 tbsp. garlic juice	1 C. corn oil
1 tbsp. oregano	1 lb. fresh mushrooms
1 tbsp. thyme	

Mix all ingredients together except mushrooms. Pour mixture over mushrooms and marinate for at least 2 hours in the refrigerator. Serve with frilled toothpicks.

Apple-Cheese Wedges

Core crisp, tart red apples and cut into wedges. Dip in fruit juice to prevent discoloration. Spread with a bit of bleu cheese that has been softened with cream. Spear each wedge with a frilled toothpick. Arrange sections in circles around a whole red apple.

Ginger Cheese Balls

8 oz. pkg. cream cheese	2 to 4 tbsp. cream
2½ oz. crumbled bleu cheese	Toasted sesame seeds
2 tbsp. shredded candied ginger	or chopped pecans

Combine all ingredients except seeds or nuts. Mix well and chill. Form very small balls, then roll in chopped pecans or toasted sesame seeds.

Pineapple-Shrimp

Spear a small whole shrimp and a pineapple cube on a cocktail pick. Serve with a cheese dip.

Stuffed Gherkins

Place a whole almond in a half gherkin to form an "acorn," or stuff gherkin with a red cherry.

Soups

If you are a soup maker already, you know that it is never necessary to throw away even the smallest scraps left over from the serving dish after a meal. Homemade stock of celery, carrots, and onions is simple to make and the perfect base for many soups, and can be easily stored in the freezer until ready to be used.

The hot, savory liquid puts the stomach in a good humor immediately. But the majority of soups are much more than just appetizers; they are rich in food value. Most nutritious are the cream soups, which contain both milk and butter in addition to the vegetables which give them their flavor.

Chowder is a special kind of cream soup which contains portions of solid foods. Fish and clam chowders are the originals, but chowders are often made with vegetables such as corn, potatoes, spinach, and cabbage. Yes, they are a substantial food, and a good-sized bowlful is a hearty luncheon main dish.

Clear soups are made from meat or vegetable stock. Vegetable soup sometimes contains a meat stock, but its chief food value is the vegetables it contains.

Soups are most mouthwatering when served with a garnish, such as a few croutons floating on top, a sprinkling of parsley, or sour cream with grated carrots.

Wild Game Stock

1 game carcass with any meat attached	6 sprigs parsley
2 onions, sliced	1 sprig thyme
2 carrots, sliced	1 bay leaf
2 to 3 stalks celery, sliced	8 peppercorns

Put the carcass of the game bird into a pan with the sliced vegetables, herbs, and seasoning. Cover with water and bring slowly to a boil, then skim off any scum that rises to the surface and simmer until well flavored and reduced in quantity. Strain and use or freeze for later use.

Fish Stock

½ lb. fish backbones and skins	1 bay leaf
1 onion, sliced	6 to 7 C. water
2 small carrots, sliced	Juice of 2 lemons
2 stalks celery	Salt and pepper to taste
6 sprigs parsley	

Use backbones from white sole, turbot, or halibut, preferably, and the skins if available. Put these in a pan with the sliced onion, carrot, celery, herbs, and water. Add lemon juice, salt, and pepper. Bring very slowly to a boil and simmer for 30 to 40 minutes until the liquid has reduced and is well flavored. Strain and cool. Use at once or freeze for later use.

Rich Brown Beef Stock

3 lb. veal bones	4 carrots
3 lb. meaty beef bones, including a bone with marrow	4 stalks celery
	6 qt. water
2 lb. lean beef (in one piece for boiled beef or cut into pieces)	Salt to taste
	10 peppercorns
	2 bay leaves
3 to 4 onions, unpeeled, or 2 onions and 2 leeks	A few mushroom stalks or peelings

Get butcher to break bones. Put them into a pan with the beef and a little beef marrow or good dripping. Heat the pan, and as the bones and meat brown, stir and keep from burning. Remove meat and bones and keep warm while browning the vegetables. Return the bones and meat to pan; cover with water. Add herbs, salt, peppercorns, and mushroom peelings or stems if available.

Bring to a boil. Skim frequently during the first hour, then cover pan and simmer for 2 to 3 hours, by which time the stock should be well flavored and a good brown color. (If the meat is a large piece and is to be used as boiled beef, it can be removed after 2 hours and the stock simmered without it for remaining cooking time.)

Strain the stock and let cool. Then skim off the fat which will form a crust on top. If the stock is not required for a day or two, do not remove fat until just before using, as it acts as a protective seal. Keep in a refrigerator or freezer.

Chicken Stock

1 boiling chicken with giblets	6 to 8 sprigs parsley
2 onions, sliced	1 sprig tarragon
4 stalks celery, sliced	1 small sprig thyme
2 to 3 carrots, sliced	6 peppercorns
1 thin sliver lemon rind	1 tsp. salt
1 bay leaf	

Put a cut-up boiling chicken into a large pot with sliced vegetables. Add the herbs and seasoning. Cover with water and bring slowly to a boil. Then cover pan and simmer for 2 hours until all the flavor is in the soup.

Strain and let cool. When cold, skim fat from the top and use the stock. The stock can also be stored in a deep freeze.

Vegetable Stock

3 medium onions, unpeeled	1 tbsp. butter or oil
3 medium carrots, peeled	2 to 3 qt. water
2 leeks, white part only	6 peppercorns
4 to 5 stalks celery	1 bay leaf
1 small turnip, peeled	4 to 6 sprigs parsley

Cut up the vegetables and brown until golden in a little butter or oil. Add water, herbs, and seasoning. Bring to a boil and simmer for 1½ to 2 hours, by which time the stock should be well flavored. Strain and cool. Use for soups or sauces calling for vegetable stock.

Mixed Household Stock

1½ lb. onions, carrots, celery, chopped	6 sprigs parsley
2 pounds mixed raw or cooked beef, veal, and/or chicken bones	1 sprig thyme
A little oil	A few mushroom stalks or peelings
1 bay leaf	6 to 8 peppercorns

Brown the raw bones and vegetables in a little hot oil. Then add the meat, bones, herbs, and mushroom peelings. Add water to cover, bring to a boil, then simmer for 1½ to 2 hours until reduced and well flavored. Strain and cool, allowing the fat to set in a solid crust on top. Use this stock quickly or keep in a refrigerator for a day or two, reboiling every day to keep it from becoming sour.

Chilled Cucumber Soup

2 C. water	1 C. sour cream
1 tbsp. natural gelatin	Juice of 1 lemon
1 C. chicken stock	2 tbsp. fresh dill, chopped fine
4 cucumbers, whirled smooth in blender	1 small onion, grated

Soften gelatin in water in a medium saucepan. Heat, stirring constantly until gelatin is dissolved, and remove from heat. Add all other ingredients and chill. Soup should be slightly thick. Serve in clear dish over ice; top each serving with sour cream and a sprig of dill.

Chilled Asparagus Soup

2 leeks, chopped	1 lb. asparagus, chopped
¼ C. butter	¼ C. flour
2 C. water	2 C. light cream
2 C. chicken stock	Salt and white pepper to taste

Sauté leeks in butter until soft in large skillet. Add water and chicken stock; bring to a boil. Add asparagus and cook 5 minutes. Stir flour into mixture until absorbed. Simmer 5 minutes. Blend soup in blender until smooth. Pour into a large bowl and stir in cream. Cover and chill at least 4 hours. Garnish and serve.

Chilled Carrot Soup

¼ C. butter	1 tsp. curry powder
1 lg. onion, chopped	Dash cayenne
1½ lb. carrots, sliced	Thin strip lemon peel
2 C. chicken stock	1 C. sour cream

Melt butter in large sauce pan and sauté onions and carrots until tender but not brown. Add chicken stock and simmer 10 minutes. Pour part of soup into blender, and add all ingredients except sour cream. Blend until smooth; add rest of soup and sour cream, blending until all are very smooth. Season to taste and chill. Serve ice cold, garnished with thin slices of carrots cut into flowers.

Cream of Carrot Soup

2 lb. carrots	½ C. whole wheat flour
2 tbsp. butter	2 C. non-fat milk
2 tbsp. onions, chopped	Salt and pepper to taste

Cook carrots in water until tender; save liquid for making vegetable stock. Mash carrots or blend in blender. Melt butter and sauté onions until clear; add flour, stir in milk, season, and simmer until creamy. Serve hot with a sprig of parsley for garnish.

Cream of Celery Soup

3 C. celery, sliced, with leaves	¼ C. butter
1 whole onion, peeled	¼ C. unbleached flour
2 C. boiling water	5 C. non-fat milk
Salt to taste	2 tsp. chopped parsley

Place celery and onion into saucepan; add water and salt. Cover and simmer until tender, about 5 minutes. Remove whole onion. Melt butter in another saucepan; blend in flour, add milk, and stir constantly over heat until sauce thickens. Stir in cooked celery and liquid. Garnish with parsley.

Cream of Corn Soup

5 C. fresh corn, cut from cob	3 C. non-fat milk
½ C. celery, chopped very fine	3 tbsp. butter
1 C. water	Salt and pepper to taste

Blend corn and celery in blender until smooth. Cook in water until mixture is creamy. Add all other ingredients and simmer 25 minutes. Serve with seasoned croutons.

Cream of Mushroom Soup

2 lb. fresh mushrooms	1 C. evaporated milk
4 tsp. finely chopped onion	2 tbsp. butter
4 C. non-fat milk	Salt and white pepper to taste

Wash mushrooms and whirl in blender until chopped fine. Place mushrooms and onions in top of double boiler, add non-fat milk, and cook for 1 hour, stirring every 10 minutes. Add evaporated milk, butter, and seasonings. Serve very hot. Garnish with sliced mushroom caps.

Cream of Onion Soup

1 C. diced onions	2 C. evaporated milk
4 tbsp. whole wheat flour	Salt and peppercorns to taste
4 C. water	

Stir all ingredients together, put in top of double boiler, and cook for 1 hour. Stir every 10 minutes until creamy. For extra zest add a little cayenne pepper. Garnish with seasoned croutons.

Cream of Salmon Soup

2 C. canned salmon	1 tbsp. celery seed
2 C. non-fat milk	3 tbsp. whole wheat flour
¼ C. finely chopped onions	

Remove skin from salmon and crumble. Add milk, onion, celery seeds, and flour to salmon and stir well. Cook in double boiler for 45 minutes. Serve with rye crisp or herbal sticks.

Purée of Turnip Soup

4 tbsp. butter	3 tbsp. whole wheat flour
2 C. sliced young turnips	Salt and pepper to taste
1 C. sliced unpeeled	1 C. non-fat milk
white potatoes	1 tbsp. chopped parsley or paprika
1 sm. onion, sliced	3 C. white or chicken stock

Melt the butter and cook the turnips, potatoes, and onion gently until they are tender, 20 to 30 minutes. Sprinkle in a little flour and blend thoroughly. Pour on the stock and mix well before bringing to a boil. Reduce heat and simmer for 15 minutes. Put soup into electric blender until smooth. Reheat, adding seasoning and milk. Sprinkle the top with parsley or paprika.

Pea Hull Soup

6 handfuls of young pea hulls	3 C. whole wheat flour
4 shallots, finely chopped	1 bay leaf
5 C. chicken stock	1 C. tomato purée
3 to 4 sprigs parsley	Salt and pepper to taste
1 sprig fresh mint	Tomato or potato (for garnish)
2 tbsp. butter	1 tbsp. chopped parsley

Shell peas and wash hulls, reserving peas for future use. Put hulls into a pan with shallots, stock, parsley, and mint. Bring to a boil and simmer until tender, about 20 minutes. Press the pulp from the pea hulls through a sieve or food mill. Melt butter and blend in the flour. Add the purée from the hulls, the liquid in which they were cooked, and a bay leaf, blending carefully. Bring to a boil, reduce heat, and simmer for 20 to 30 minutes or until the vegetables are tender. Remove bay leaf. Put soup through a fine food mill or blend in electric blender until smooth. Reheat, adding the tomato purée, and adjust seasoning to taste. Serve hot, garnished with the chopped flesh of one peeled and seeded tomato or potato diced, cooked in a little boiling water. Sprinkle with chopped parsley.

Onion Soup Marshalls Style

3 qt. beef broth	2 carrots, grated
4 onions, chopped fine	Sour cream

Boil beef broth, onions, and carrots until tender. When serving, place one tsp. of sour cream in bowl, then add hot onion soup. Yum! Yum!

Egg Drop Soup

1 qt. chicken broth	2 eggs, well beaten
3 tbsp. soy sauce	3 tbsp. chopped parsley

Boil chicken broth, then add soy sauce and pour eggs into center of contents while still boiling. Add parsley. This soup is delightful with oriental meals.

Potato Peel Soup Marshalls Style

1 lg. onion, chopped	1 gal. water
1 C. diced celery	Grated peels from
2 carrots, grated	1 lb. fresh white potatoes
¼ lb. butter	

Sauté onions, celery, and carrots in butter until tender. Add water and potato peels. Simmer until slightly thick. Serve this as a vegetarian favorite.

Carrot Soup

12 carrots, grated	1 gal. water
2 tbsp. olive oil	1 C. milk
1 lg. onion, chopped	

Simmer carrots, olive oil, and onions in water until carrots are tender and creamy. Add milk and remove from heat. It's ready to eat.

Parsnip Soup

3 tbsp. butter	5 cups vegetable or chicken stock
1½ C. peeled and finely sliced parsnips	1 small bay leaf
1 onion, chopped	A pinch of thyme
3 tbsp. whole wheat flour	A pinch of nutmeg
	½ C. cream

Melt the butter and cook the onion and parsnips gently, with a lid on the pan to soften without browning, for 5 to 6 minutes. Remove from heat and sprinkle in flour. Then blend well. Pour on stock, mix well, and add herbs and seasonings. Bring to a boil and simmer for 20 to 30 minutes until the parsnips are tender. Remove bay leaf. Blend soup in electric blender until smooth. Return soup to pan; adjust seasoning and reheat, adding cream.

Green Bean Soup

2 to 3 tbsp. butter	Salt and pepper to taste
4 shallots, finely chopped	2 lb. fresh green beans
1 clove garlic, crushed	1 tsp. chopped or dried summer savory
2 tbsp. whole wheat flour	
4 C. veal stock	

Melt the butter and cook the shallots and garlic for 5 to 6 minutes in a covered pan. Add the flour and blend in smoothly. Pour on stock and mix well. When smooth, bring to a boil, stirring constantly. Add salt and pepper.

String the beans and cut in slanting slices or break in half, depending on their size. Add to the soup with savory and cook for 25 minutes or until beans are tender. Strain the soup, saving and keeping warm a few pieces of bean for garnish. Put remaining soup and beans through a food mill or blend until smooth in electric blender. Reheat soup, adjusting seasoning to taste.

Parsley Soup

3 C. fresh parsley	3 C. vegetable stock
4 tbsp. butter	Salt and pepper to taste
1 onion, chopped	Pinch of nutmeg
2 stalks celery, chopped	1 bay leaf
3 tbsp. whole wheat flour	Sour cream

Coarsely chop the parsley including stems, which are full of flavor. Melt butter and cook onions and celery gently for a few minutes without browning. Sprinkle in flour and mix well. Pour on stock and bring slowly to a boil, blending smoothly. Add the chopped parsley and salt, pepper, nutmeg, and bay leaf. Simmer for 25 minutes.

This soup can be served as it is, or blended in an electric blender. Reheat soup, pour into soup bowls, and serve over a spoonful of sour cream in each bowl. Garnish with paprika and croutons.

Yogurt Soup

2 pts. yogurt	1 tsp. dill
3 cucumbers, chopped	1 clove garlic, diced
3 tbsp. lemon juice	1 tsp. lemon rind

Place all ingredients in blender container and blend until creamy smooth. Chill.

Black Bean Soup

1½ lb. black turtle beans	1 tsp. salt
2 green peppers, including seeds and membrane, chopped	1 tsp. basil
2 medium onions, chopped	1 tsp. cumin
2 cloves garlic	6 tsp. butter

Soak beans overnight to save cooking time. Cook beans until tender in two quarts of water. Blend all other ingredients in blender and add the mixture to beans and simmer 1 hour or more. Add more water if soup is too thick.

Cauliflower Soup

1 medium cauliflower	3 tbsp. whole wheat flour
1 bay leaf	¼ tsp. mace
3 tbsp. butter	1 tbsp. chopped chervil
1 onion, chopped	½ C. cream
1 medium unpeeled potato, chopped	Grated cheese
	5 C. non-fat milk

Divide well-washed cauliflower into flowerets and cut the hard stalk and leaves into small pieces. Cook the cauliflower in boiling salted water. Meanwhile, melt the butter, add the onions and potato, and cook gently for 5 to 6 minutes, stirring to prevent browning. Sprinkle in flour and blend smoothly. Pour in milk and mix well before bringing to a boil. Add the cauliflower, then reduce heat and simmer gently until potatoes and cauliflower are just tender. Put the soup into an electric blender and blend until smooth. Add mace and cream. Sprinkle with chopped chervil and serve grated cheese separately.

Split Pea Soup

1 C. split peas	¼ C. parsley
1½ qt. water	1 tsp. olive oil
1 lg. onion, chopped	1 tsp. oregano
3 stalks celery, chopped	1 tsp. basil
4 carrots, grated fine	Vegetable salt to taste

Combine all ingredients. Bring to boil, cover, and reduce heat; simmer for 2 hours. If you want a smoother consistency, blend soup in blender.

Fresh Pea Soup

4 C. shelled May peas	4 tbsp. melted butter
2 C. water	4 tbsp. whole wheat flour
¼ C. chopped scallions	4 C. non-fat milk

Cook peas in water for about 10 minutes, until tender. Blend the cooked peas in blender, add scallions, and blend 1 minute more. Melt butter and stir in flour; cook gently 2 or 3 minutes. Slowly stir in milk until thickened. Add the pea mixture and stir together. Keep soup hot in a double boiler. Garnish if desired.

Lentil Soup I

3 C. red or green lentils	4 peppercorns
1 lg. onion, chopped	1 tbsp. savory
4 tbsp. olive oil	2 tsp. chopped parsley
1 clove garlic, chopped	4 qt. water
3 stalks celery, chopped	Salt to taste
3 carrots, grated	

Combine all above ingredients and simmer until lentils are tender. To cream the soup, blend in electric blender. Garnish with whole wheat croutons.

Lentil Soup II

3 C. green or brown lentils	4 stalks celery, chopped fine
1 lg. onion, chopped	Vegetable salt to taste
3 fresh tomatoes, chopped	3 qt. water
2 tbsp. parsley	½ C. whole wheat flour
1 tbsp. white pepper	¼ C. butter or corn oil
1 C. grated carrots	

Cook lentils and vegetables together with seasoning. Cook flour and butter slowly until golden brown, on the dark side of golden. When lentils are tender, add lentil mixture to flour mixture and simmer 30 to 40 more minutes. Stir often to keep from sticking.

Cabbage Soup

4 unpeeled white potatoes	1½ qt. water
1 lg. green cabbage	Salt and peppercorns to taste
1 onion, chopped fine	½ C. olive oil

Wash and chop potatoes and cabbage and blend at medium speed. Then combine all ingredients in pot and simmer for 1 hour.

Black Bread Soup

1 loaf or 10 slices pumpernickel bread	1 lb. Swiss cheese, cubed
6 C. hot non-fat milk	Nutmeg
¼ C. butter	

Toast bread; cut each slice into 5 or 6 sticks. For each serving, place 5-6 toast sticks in a mug, add some cheese and butter, and pour hot milk over. Sprinkle with nutmeg.

Tomato Soup Supreme

12 summer red tomatoes	4 stalks celery, chopped
4 tbsp. whole wheat flour	4 tbsp. butter
4 tbsp. soy flour	Salt and pepper to taste
½ onion, chopped	

Place all ingredients except salt and pepper in blender. Blend for 3 minutes. Simmer for 25 minutes; season. Serve with wheat thins and grated cheese.

Creamy Barley Soup

¼ C. parsnips, chopped	4 tomatoes, peeled and chopped
2 C. medium grated carrots	2 C. barley
2 medium onions, chopped fine	3 qt. water

Sauté the vegetables in a little peanut oil until slightly brown. Add water, barley, and salt to taste; cook for 25 minutes.

Pumpkin Soup

3 tbsp. whole wheat flour	1 lb. Swiss cheese
1 qt. chicken stock	3 tbsp. melted butter
1 qt. fresh pumpkin,	Vegetable salt to taste
whirled in blender until creamy	1 clove garlic, minced

Stir flour into all other ingredients and simmer slowly for 2 hours, stirring constantly; if soup becomes too thick, add a little more stock. If you have any of this soup left over, add a little soy sauce to it and broil fresh fish in it.
This will have your family wondering why the fish is so good. Your friends will beg you for the recipe. My guests at the Marshalls sure do.

Vegetable Cream Soup

1 lb. broccoli	1 lb. Brussels sprouts
1 lb. turnip root	Vegetable salt
1 lb. May peas	

Steam vegetables until tender or use leftover vegetables. Blend in blender and heat in double boiler. Very tasty.

Spinach Soup

2 lb. fresh spinach	1 bay leaf
3 tbsp. butter	Salt and pepper
1 onion, finely chopped	Squeeze or two of lemon juice
3 tbsp. whole wheat flour	¼ to ½ tsp. powdered mace
4 C. vegetable stock	½ C. cream
3 to 4 sprigs parsley	

Wash the spinach thoroughly; drain and shake off excess water. Melt butter and cook the onion and spinach gently until the spinach has softened and become limp, without browning. Sprinkle in flour and blend smoothly.
Add the stock. Bring soup to a boil, stirring constantly. Then add parsley and bay leaf. Reduce heat and simmer 10 to 12 minutes. Do not overcook, as this spoils the green color and fresh flavor. Put soup through a fine food mill or blend until smooth in an electric blender. Reheat, adding a little lemon juice. Adjust seasoning and add the mace. Stir in the cream just before serving.

Watercress Soup

3 bunches fresh watercress	1 bay leaf
3 tbsp. butter	2 C. non-fat milk
1 white potato, sliced	¼ tsp. powdered mace
1 sm. onion, finely chopped	Salt to taste
2 tbsp whole wheat flour	¼ C. chopped parsley
1 C. stock	Sour cream

Wash and pick over the watercress, discarding any yellow leaves. Reserve enough green top sprigs to make the final garnish and chop the remaining cress roughly. Melt the butter and cook the potato and onion together for 2 to 3 minutes before adding the chopped watercress. Continue cooking for 3 to 4 minutes, stirring constantly to prevent browning. Sprinkle in flour and blend well. Add stock and blend together before bringing to a boil. Add bay leaf and seasonings, reduce heat, and simmer until the potato is tender, about 20 minutes. Remove bay leaf. Put soup into electric blender and blend until smooth. Return soup to pan and reheat gently. At the same time heat milk in a separate pan. When almost at boiling point, pour into watercress mixture. Adjust seasoning, adding mace. Serve with a spoon of sour cream in each cup and the reserved watercress sprigs on top.

Lettuce Soup

2 to 3 heads lettuce	4 C. chicken stock
3 tbsp. butter	1 C. evaporated milk
1 sm. onion or 6 to 8 young	4 sprigs parsley
green onions, finely chopped	2 sprigs mint
2 tbsp. whole wheat flour	2 tbsp. honey

Chop the well-washed lettuce coarsely. Melt butter and soften the lettuce and onion gently in a covered pan for 5 to 6 minutes without browning. Sprinkle in the flour and blend smoothly; add stock, parsley, mint, and honey. When smooth, bring to a boil, stirring constantly. Reduce heat and simmer for 15 minutes.

Put soup into electric blender and blend until smooth or put through food mill or fine sieve. Reheat soup in clean pan. Meanwhile, heat the milk in another pan and add when on the point of boiling. This lightens the texture of the soup. If serving hot, serve with bread croutons; if cold, with brown bread and butter.

Gazpacho Soup

1 C. garbanzo beans	2 tsp. salt
1 qt. water	¼ tsp. pepper
6 medium tomatoes, peeled and minced	⅛ tsp. cayenne
	1¼ C. tomato juice
2 medium cucumbers, minced	Diced bell pepper and
1 medium onion, minced	green onions (optional)
¼ C. olive oil	Sour cream
3 tbsp. cider vinegar	Chopped parsley

Cook beans in water until tender; refrigerate overnight. Simmer with all other ingredients, 45 minutes. In each bowl place a spoonful of sour cream; pour warm soup over, and sprinkle with parsley. Also a great cold salad-soup for hot days when tomatoes and cucumbers are ripe.

Chicken Rice Soup

1 gal. chicken stock	1 tsp. salt
1 C. onions, chopped	1 C. chopped, cooked chicken
1 C. celery, diced	¼ lb. butter
½ lb. brown rice	½ C. whole wheat flour

Add vegetables and rice to stock and simmer until tender. Add seasonings and chicken. In a separate pan, melt butter, stir in flour, add hot soup gradually. Stir until smooth.

Artichoke Soup

2 C. water	3 tbsp. butter
1 tsp. lemon juice	1 onion, finely sliced
1 bay leat	1 stalk celery, finely sliced
3 to 4 sprigs parsley	4 tbsp. whole wheat flour
1 tsp. salt	2 C. milk
Pepper and powdered mace to taste	2 egg yolks
3 C. sliced Jerusalem artichokes	½ C. cream

Put the water, lemon juice, bay leaf, parsley, and seasoning into a pan and add the artichokes. Bring to a boil and simmer until tender, about 10 to 15 minutes. Melt the butter and cook the onion and celery slowly with lid on pan until soft. Do not allow to brown. Sprinkle in flour and blend well.

When artichokes are tender, strain the liquid on to the onion mixture and blend well. Remove bay leaf and parsley sprigs and add these to soup. Mix in artichokes and bring to a boil, stirring constantly. Blend thoroughly in an eletric blender until creamy. Return to pan and reheat.

At the same time, in another pan, heat the milk to just below boiling point. Pour into artichoke soup and whisk together (adding hot rather than cold milk makes a lighter and more delicate soup). Mix the egg yolks and cream thoroughly, add a few spoonfuls of hot soup, mix well, then strain into soup, stirring constantly. Reheat soup.

Chestnut Soup

2 lbs. chestnuts	1 tbsp. parsley, chopped
3 tbsp. butter	A pinch of thyme
1 large onion, sliced	1 bay leaf
2 small carrots, sliced	A pinch of nutmeg
1 stalk celery, sliced	1 C. cream
4 to 5 C. chicken stock	

Make a small slit in the top of each nut and place in a well-greased pan in a 375° oven for 12 to 15 minutes to loosen both outer and inner skin. Remove both skins and reserve nutmeat. Melt the butter and add the onion, carrots, and celery. Mix well over gentle heat before adding the chestnuts. Cover the pan and cook for 3 to 4 minutes, shaking the pan occasionally. Add the stock, herbs, and seasoning, and simmer for 20 to 30 minutes, or until the chestnuts and vegetables are tender.

Remove the bay leaf; put soup into electric blender and blend until smooth, or put through a fine food mill. Return to pan and reheat soup. Season to taste. Add the cream just before serving or put a spoon of cream in each soup cup.

Cayce Chicken Soup

2 sets chicken giblets	6 peppercorns
1 lg. onion, sliced	Salt
2 to 3 carrots, sliced	2 tbsp. butter
2 to 3 stalks celery, sliced	1½ tsp. whole wheat flour
Chicken skin and carcass	1 tbsp. butter
5 C. water	2 chicken livers
4 to 5 parsley stalks, 1 sprig of	2 tbsp. parsley, chopped
thyme, 1 bay leaf (tied together)	

Wash the chicken giblets, removing the livers. Reserve these for garnish. Put the onion, carrots, and celery into a pan with the giblets and any skin or carcass from the chicken. Add the water, herbs, peppercorns, and some salt. Bring slowly to a boil, skimming off any scum that rises to the top. Reduce heat and simmer for 1½ hours, until the vegetables are tender and the giblets well cooked. Remove skin and carcass or strain soup into another pan.

Melt the butter and blend in the flour. Strain into the chicken stock, blend thoroughly, and bring to a boil, stirring constantly. Cook for a few minutes.

Cook the chicken livers gently in 1 tbsp. butter for about 5 to 8 minutes, depending on their size. Chop livers roughly and divide between soup cups before pouring on hot soup. Sprinkle with chopped parsley.

Chicken Gumbo Soup

6 C. strong chicken stock	3 tbsp. safflower oil
2 C. chopped chicken meat	1 sm. onion, chopped
1 C. fresh cut corn	1 C. cooked brown rice
1 C. fresh or frozen okra	1 tsp. chopped tarragon
4 ripe tomatoes, peeled	3 tsp. chopped parsley
and diced	Seasonings to taste

Combine all above ingredients and bring to a boil. Simmer for 30 minutes. Keep covered, stirring every 10 minutes. Garnish and serve.

Yellow Pea Soup

3 C. yellow peas	2 carrots, grated
6 C. water	1 lg. potato, grated
2 onions, chopped	2 bay leaves
1 C. chopped celeriac or celery	2 C. chicken stock (optional)

Rinse and soak peas overnight in refrigerator. Don't throw water away; use as part of the 6 cups. Add all other ingredients and bring to a boil. Lower heat and cook 2 hours until rich and creamy. If needed, add more water. Keep covered when cooking. Stir every 15 minutes or so.

Cabbage-Tomato Soup

1 green cabbage, shredded	2 tsp. chopped dill
2 sm. leeks, sliced	1 sm. onion, chopped
6 fresh red tomatoes, peeled and diced	3 tbsp. olive oil
	Seasoning to taste
1 bay leaf	3 qts. water

Combine all ingredients in large pot and bring to boil. Lower heat and simmer for 40 minutes. Serve a bowl of wheat croutons with this soup.

Cheese Soup

4 C. grated mild Cheddar cheese	4 C. non-fat milk
1 C. grated Monterey Jack cheese	1 bay leaf
3 tbsp. grated Sardo or Parmesan cheese	Salt to taste
1 C. grated Swiss cheese	1 sprig parsley

Place all ingredients in top of double boiler and stir every 5 minutes with wire whip, cooking time shouldn't be over 30 minutes. Garnish with parsley. This is Dr. Harold Reilly's favorite; he always has a second helping.

Scotch Broth

2 lb. lamb necks	4 carrots, diced
3 qt. water	2 leeks, sliced
2 bay leaves	6 stalks celery, chopped
2 lg. onions, chopped	1 C. barley, soaked overnight
2 cloves	

Boil lamb necks, 1 onion, bay leaves, cloves, 3 stalks of celery, and 2 carrots, about one hour in 3 quarts of water. Strain, pick meat off bones and place back in stock; add barley and bring to a boil adding all other ingredients. Simmer until vegetables are tender, about 15 minutes.

Chicken Noodle Soup

4 to 5 C. well-flavored clear chicken stock	4 tbsp. fine noodles
	2 tbsp. finely chopped parsley

Bring stock to a boil, add noodles, stirring constantly, and boil slowly for about 15 minutes or for time stated on package of noodles. Stir frequently to prevent noodles from sticking. Add seasoning to taste. Serve hot in soup cups liberally sprinkled with finely chopped parsley.

Scripture Soup

2½ qts. Proverbs 25:25	Leviticus 2:13 to taste
2 C. of Ezekiel 4:9	1 tsp. Exodus 16:31
1 lb. of Leviticus 3:7	

Simmer for 2 hours, covered. Serve as Solomon did in I Kings 4:15.

Salads and Dressings

A green salad, prepared properly, is an exciting addition to any meal, but as with any dish, a lack of loving care in its preparation will simply ruin the end result.

Strictly speaking, a green salad consists only of greens and a carefully seasoned dressing. Fresh vegetables may also be added to a green salad, but when little or no extras are to be added, it is best to choose an assortment of fresh greens.

We have a lovely garden at the Marshalls, which we are very proud of. Because of this, our vegetables are not only local, but are garden fresh and require no refrigeration.

A vegetable salad, of course, can be only as good as the vegetables that go into it. Use fresh vegetables such as tomatoes, zucchini, cauliflower, cucumbers, broccoli, asparagus, carrots, radishes, and both red and white cabbage.

Use good vibrations and imagination in combining your salad. I find that the Edgar Cayce Readings are very helpful in this. Cayce said to combine one root vegetable with two above ground vegetables, keeping them harmonious in color, texture, and flavor.

Meat, seafood, and poultry salads are the hearty members of the salad family. They are sometimes served as full-meal salads or as the main luncheon course, yet in small servings they make excellent appetizer salads.

A fruit salad bar is an eye-catching addition to any buffet table. Serve platters of assorted fruits, attractively arranged in rows: thin slices of peeled fresh pineapples, slices of oranges and grapefruits, grapes, sliced pears, bananas, avocados, and melons.

Offer a choice of dressings, then allow your guests or family to combine their own salads. A good salad makes a better meal.

Mung Bean Sprout Salad

2 C. mung bean sprouts
2 tbsp. olive or vegetable oil
½ C. tarragon vinegar
4 drops garlic juice

2 tbsp. chopped parsley
Juice of 1 lemon
3 tbsp. honey

Toss together lightly until juices are well mixed. This salad needs no dressing.

Bleu Cheese-Vegetable Salad

1 head endive
1 head iceberg lettuce
1 head cauliflower
1 lg. Spanish red onion

½ C. stuffed olives, cut in half
½ C. ripe olives, pitted
   and cut in half
1 C. crumbled bleu cheese

Break lettuce and endive in small to medium pieces. Separate cauliflower into flowerets. Slice and arrange over greens. Cut the onion into thin rings and place over the flowerets. Sprinkle the bleu cheese and olives over all. No dressing is needed.

Raw Broccoli Salad

1 lg. Bermuda onion
2 lb. fresh broccoli
1 pt. cherry tomatoes, cut in halves

1 head fresh cauliflower,
   cut in small rosettes

Slice broccoli stalks into thin strips; cut cauliflower in rosettes. Toss lightly together and serve with creamy horseradish dressing.

Cabbage and Raisin Salad

4 C. shredded cabbage
1 C. seedless raisins

½ C. cole slaw dressing
Crisp lettuce leaves

Gently toss together the first three ingredients. Spoon on crisp, individual lettuce leaves, and garnish the top with a few raisins.

Carrot and Raisin Salad

3 C. shredded carrots
1 C. seedless raisins
¾ C. sour cream

½ C. honey
Bibb lettuce
1 C. fresh pineapple chunks

Toss first four ingredients together. Serve on Bibb lettuce leaves; garnish with fresh pineapple chunks.

Vegetable Coleslaw

1 head cabbage, shredded fine
1 lb. fresh broccoli,
   including stems, chopped fine
1 lb. carrots, grated fine

2 C. sour cream
2 tbsp. lemon juice
¾ C. honey
10 radishes, grated fine

Mix all ingredients together. Line a bowl with Bibb lettuce so that leaves overlap edges; place coleslaw in the center and garnish with radish rosettes or carrot flowers.

Fruit Coleslaw

1 head cabbage, shredded fine
2 C. finely chopped dried apples
1 C. finely chopped dried peaches
1 C. crushed cooked pineapple

1 C. grated coconut
1 C. seedless raisins
2 C. yogurt

Do not precook dried fruit; it will reconstitute in the liquid of the slaw. Mix all ingredients except yogurt, reserving ¼ cup each of raisins and coconut. Add yogurt and toss gently. Place slaw in center of platter and surround with overlapping endive leaves. Garnish with reserved coconut and raisins. Chill 2 hours before serving.

Cucumber Yogurt Salad

A wonderful salad with a touch of mint.

6 lg. cucumbers	2 lg. garlic cloves, finely minced
3 C. plain yogurt	2 tbsp. finely chopped mint
½ C. chopped green onions	2 tbsp. tarragon vinegar

Score cucumbers and slice paper thin. Combine yogurt, green onions, garlic, mint, and vinegar. Add cucumbers; toss gently with a wooden spoon. Cover. Refrigerate 1 hour to allow flavors to mingle. Garnish with mint or pimiento.

Guacamole Salad

2 avocados	2 tbsp. cream cheese
Juice of ½ lemon	Cayenne pepper to taste

Cut 2 avocados in half, remove seed, and scoop out pulp. Save the shells; place the pulp in a blender with a little lemon juice, cream cheese, and cayenne pepper. Place the mixture back in the avocado shells and garnish with mint leaves, pimiento, or chives.

Raw May Pea Salad

2 C. fresh May peas	1 tsp. fresh dill weed
2 scallions, sliced	1 small carrot, grated
1 C. sunflower seeds	

Toss all of the ingredients together. Serve in a well-chilled bowl with a salad dressing of your choice.

Crisp Spinach Salad

1 lb. fresh spinach,
    broken in small pieces
1 clove garlic, minced
2 sliced scallions, tops and all

4 ripe tomatoes, cut in wedges
½ C. vegetable oil
¼ C. vinegar

Toss together and garnish with hard-boiled eggs.

Avocado Salad

Cut avocado in half and remove the seeds. Dip the avocado halves in lemon juice to prevent darkening. Stuff the halves with chopped chicken or chicken salad mixture. Serve with wheat thins.

    The avocado seed makes a nice houseplant, and is easy to grow. Place 3 toothpicks in the seed and put the small end of the seed in a cup of water. Do not cover the entire seed with water. When sprouts begin to show, plant in regular houseplant soil.

Banana Finger Salad

1 head of endive, rinsed
8 ripe bananas
½ C. grated coconut

½ C. wheat germ
½ C. sesame seeds

Cover the entire surface of a platter with endive. Slice bananas lengthwise and cut in half. Take each piece of banana and dip the cut side alternately in coconut, wheat germ, and sesame seeds. Arrange decoratively on the dish, allowing family or guests to help themselves. The children will love this as an after-school snack.

Fresh Berry Bowl

1 qt. fresh strawberries
1 qt. fresh blueberries

1 qt. fresh gooseberries
Lettuce

Wash and clean all berries. Mix together and serve in a bowl lined with lettuce. Set picks close by and watch the berries disappear.

Cantaloupe Ball Salad

Ball 2 fresh cantaloupes with a melon baller, and garnish with fresh strawberries. Leave the stems on the strawberries; serve with your favorite fruit dressing or a little honey and lemon juice. Chill.

Cantaloupe Supreme

1 cantaloupe
1 qt. fresh strawberries,
    leaves and stems removed

6 lemon wedges

Peel a whole cantaloupe and slice it into 6 medum rings. Place a ring on an individual lettuce leaf and fill with fresh whole strawberries. Garnish each with a lemon wedge.

Fresh Citrus Salad I

3 oranges, peeled
2 grapefruits, peeled
2 fresh pineapples. Select
    a pineapple with yellow
    between the grooves

Bibb lettuce leaves
1 C. grated coconut

Slice oranges and grapefruits in opposite directions from fibers. They will look like wheels. Peel, core, and cube the pineapples. Place Bibb lettuce on a medium-sized platter with pineapple chunks in the center. Alternate orange and grapefruit slices around the chunks. Sprinkle coconut over the pineapple.

Citrus Salad II

Skin unbroken whole or half sections of oranges or grapefruit or both. Arrange the sections on greens around a center of dates, figs, and nut halves.

Citrus Salad III

Lettuce, endive,
or other leafy greens
Oranges, peeled and
cut into segments

Pimientos
Banana peppers
Green peppers

Use these ingredients according to taste and in suitable proportions for the number of people being served. Arrange greens on individual plates. Place the orange segments in a circle on the greens. In the center of the circle, place long slices of green pepper, pimiento, and banana peppers.

Coconut Fruit Bowl Salad

½ watermelon, sliced lengthwise
1 head leaf lettuce
1 honeydew melon

2 cantaloupes
1 pkg. grated coconut

Scoop out fruit in balls with a melon baller. Save the shell of the watermelon half and line the bottom and sides with leaf lettuce. Set aside. Place all of the fruit balls in a large bowl and toss with grated coconut. Gently slide the fruit mixture into the watermelon shell. Garnish with fresh mint leaves.

Dandelion Salad

1 clove garlic
1 lb. tender dandelion greens
¾ C. chopped black olives

½ C. olive oil
Juice of one fresh lemon

Rub a bowl with the garlic. Add the rest of the ingredients and toss with olive oil and lemon juice.

Grape Salad

6 C. grape juice	6 C. cut and seeded red grapes
5 tbsp. natural gelatin	4 C. watermelon balls
¼ C. lemon juice	½ C. red wine (optional)
4 tbsp. honey	Sour cream

In a saucepan, heat grape juice. Add gelatin and stir. Add lemon juice and honey. Chill until slightly thickened. Add fruit, folding in. Mold and serve with sour cream over a bed of lettuce.

May Salad

1 pt. whipping cream	1 lb. seedless white grapes
1 qt. fresh strawberries, leaves and stems removed	Honey to taste

Whip the whipping cream until light and fluffy. Add honey the last few seconds of whipping process. Fold strawberries and grapes into cream. Serve on salad plates with lettuce leaves and garnish with one large strawberry and 4 or 5 grapes.

Peaches and Cream Salad

4 oz. cream cheese	8 fresh peaches, pitted and cut in half
1 C. chopped pecans	
Bibb lettuce	

Cut the cheese into 8 equal parts; form into balls and roll them in chopped pecans. Place a cheese ball into each peach half and close with the other half. If the peaches are not served at once, roll them in lemon juice, and chill them in a tightly closed container. Serve on Bibb lettuce and slice for finger food. If left whole, the peaches may be decorated with stems and leaves. This makes a very nice centerpiece when small bunches of fresh grapes are added.

Pear Salad I

3 lg. oranges	Lemon juice
2 lg. pears	Salad greens

Peel and section oranges; slice each section in half. Core pears; cut into 6 wedges. Sprinkle the pears with lemon juice to keep them from turning brown. Arrange greens on a salad plate and top with pear and orange slices. Serve with your favorite fruit dressing.

Pear Salad II

4 fresh pears	2 C. cottage cheese
1 head iceberg lettuce	

Peel and core pears; cut each in half. Break lettuce into small pieces. Place cottage cheese in the center of the lettuce. Slice pears all around. This salad needs no dressing.

Prune Salad

2 C. chopped prunes	2 C. shredded Cheddar cheese
2 C. chopped walnuts	2 C. yogurt
4 C. chopped figs	

Combine fruits, nuts, and cheese in large mixing bowl and toss gently with yogurt.

Pineapple Bowls

1 fresh pineapple	2 oranges, sectioned
1 pt. fresh strawberries	

Cut a pineapple in half leaving the leafy top intact. Hollow out the halves, leaving a shell ½ inch thick. Cut out the core and throw it away. Cube the remaining pineapple; mix it with the orange sections and fresh strawberries, and refill the shells. Chill. Trim with fresh mint, if you like.

Watermelon Basket Salad

1 plump short watermelon	2 cantaloupes
2 honeydew melons	Grapes

Chill watermelon. Slice off top third of watermelon and set aside. Use the larger piece for the fruit holder. With melon baller, ball both pieces of the watermelon, the honeydews, and the cantaloupes.

Mark big scallops around the top edge, using the rim of a small glass as the outline, or just cut it in zig-zag fashion all around. Fill the watermelon bowl with the melon balls in any fashion you choose. Tuck in grapes, mint, or any type of lettuce leaf, if you desire. Set a bunch of frilled toothpicks close by and watch the fruit disappear.

Chicken Salad Mixture

This is a great American favorite and can be served in a lot of ways. But one rule that should be remembered is to keep the proportions of chicken two to one of all other ingredients combined.

Cook chicken and save stock for soup and sauces. Chop celery, hard-boiled eggs, and a little pimiento and add to your favorite salad dressing.

This basic salad mixture can then be mixed two to one with any of the following: Water chestnuts and bean, wheat, lentil, or alfalfa sprouts; I use a peanut oil and vinegar dressing with these. Nut meats and melted butter. Fresh diced cucumber and sour cream. Pomegranate seeds served on wheat thins. Chopped fresh capers. Crushed pineapple made by whirling fresh pineapple in blender. Cream cheese and garlic. Chopped cheese sprinkled over green salad with chicken salad mixture, and topped with whole wheat croutons.

Cold Roast Beef Salad

If you've been wondering what to do with leftover roast beef, here is a suggestion. Chop the beef in a blender, add horseradish dressing, and mix for a delicious salad. Serve on a bed of greens or as a sandwich spread. Cooked turkey, duck, or lamb may be substituted for the beef in this recipe.

Corned Beef Salad

Cooked corned beef, diced
Hard-boiled eggs, chopped
Fresh celery leaves, chopped
Fresh green pepper, chopped

Honey
Vinegar
Sour cream

Use these ingredients according to taste and in suitable proportions for the number of people being served. Combine the diced corned beef with the chopped eggs, celery leaves, and green pepper. Mix the honey and vinegar until sweet-tart; add the sour cream and pour over the meat and vegetable mixture. This also makes a great sandwich spread.

Crab Meat Louis

Lettuce
Crab meat

Louis dressing
Hard-boiled eggs

Place lettuce leaves on the bottom of a dish or bowl. Pile crab meat on the lettuce leaves. Add Louis sauce and garnish with sliced hard-boiled eggs.

Shrimp Louis

Shrimp
Lettuce

Louis dressing
Tomato wedges

Shell and clean fresh shrimp and steam for 5 minutes. Place lettuce leaves on the bottom of a dish or bowl. Pile shrimp on the lettuce leaves. Add Louis sauce. Lobster meat can be substituted for shrimp. Garnish with tomato wedges.

Molded Salads

Molded salads, aspic, and mousse are glorified and tempting when made with leftovers. They are second only to a well-prepared souffle. Well-combined leftovers result in a dish that is sometimes as good as one prepared from delicacies. There is a further advantage to the busy cook because they can be prepared in advance, and chilled until ready to serve. Never freeze these salads; the gelatin will hold them together in refrigeration.

Clear aspics are lovely coolers on hot summer evenings. Always serve them on a well-chilled platter or plate. For a quivery effect, unmold the aspic onto a dish that is seated in crushed ice.

Unmolding gelatin salads: Individual salads may be be unmolded onto salad greens. Large molds are best on a serving platter that is covered with greens to prevent breaking of the mold. First moisten the platter with a few drops of cold water, then it will be easier to slide the mold to the center of the platter if you wish. Only pure gelatin is used in recipes in this book. Note: Fresh pineapple will not jell.

Mint Gelatin for Fruit Salads

1 C. boiling water	¼ C. crushed mint leaves

Pour water over mint leaves; allow to steep for 5 minutes. Drain. Use this water as part or all of the gelatin water when mixing gelatin salad.

Cranberry Ring Salad

2 C. fresh cranberries	½ C. chopped nuts
1½ C. cold water	¾ C. diced celery
1 C. honey	Lettuce
2 tbsp. gelatin	

Wash cranberries, add 1 C. cold water. Cook until tender. Add honey and cook for 5 minutes. Soften gelatin in ½ cup cold water; dissolve in hot cranberries. Chill until mixture begins to thicken. Add nuts and celery. Mix thoroughly. Pour into ring mold. Chill until firm. Unmold, and place on a large salad plate. Place lettuce around the salad. For variety, arrange shrimp in the center, or serve on a bed of chicory on individual plates and garnish.

Cranberry Orange Molds

2 C. fresh cranberries	3 tbsp. lemon juice
2 small oranges	1 C. boiling water
1 C. honey	Lettuce
2 tbsp. gelatin	

Wash and dry the cranberries and peel the oranges. Put uncooked cranberries and 1 orange peel through a food chopper; dice the orange pulp and add with the honey. Dissolve gelatin in boiling water and cool. Combine with lemon juice and the cranberry-orange mixture, pour into molds, and chill until firm. Unmold on lettuce and serve.

Grape Bavarian Mold

2 tbsp. plain gelatin	1 tbsp. lemon juice
2 C. grape juice	½ C. honey
⅓ C. orange juice	½ C. whipping cream

Sprinkle gelatin over ¼ cup of the cold grape juice and let stand 5 minutes. Heat in a double boiler over hot water, stirring until the gelatin dissolves. Meanwhile, combine the rest of the grape juice with the orange juice, half the lemon juice, and the honey, stirring until the honey is mixed; then stir in the gelatin mixture. Chill until thick and syrupy; then beat with a rotary beater until light and fluffy. Have cream thoroughly chilled; beat until stiff, add the rest of the lemon juice, and beat until very stiff. Fold thoroughly into grape gelatin and transfer to a mold which has been rinsed with cold water. Chill until firm. Unmold onto a chilled serving plate.

Sunshine Salad

2 tbsp. gelatin	½ tsp. salt
1¼ C. hot water	1 C. cooked crushed pineapple
1 tbsp. cider vinegar	1 C. shredded raw carrots
¼ C. honey	Crisp lettuce
1 C. fresh orange juice	Mayonnaise

Dissolve gelatin by stirring into the hot water. Add vinegar, honey, orange juice and salt; stir to mix well, then chill until syrupy. Add crushed pineapple, with its juice and the carrots. Pour the mixture into a mold that has been rubbed with salad oil, and chill until firm. Unmold onto a chilled serving plate. Serve on lettuce with mayonnaise, if desired.

Molded Vegetable Salad

2 C. water	½ C. sliced celery
2 tbsp. gelatin	1 C. diced Monterey Jack cheese,
1 tsp. salt	about ⅓ lb.
Juice of 1 lemon	Lettuce
1 C. fresh May peas	Mayonnaise

Mix water with gelatin and heat to boiling point, stirring constantly. Add salt and lemon juice and chill until thick and syrupy; then fold in peas, celery, and cheese. Turn mixture into oiled mold and chill until firm. When ready to serve, unmold onto plate lined with crisp lettuce and serve with mayonnaise, if desired.

Pineapple-Cheese Salad

3 tbsp. gelatin	1 C. honey
½ C. cold water	1 C. heavy cream, whipped
2½ C. crushed pineapple	1 C. shredded Cheddar cheese
3 tbsp. lemon juice	½ C. chopped walnuts

Soften the gelatin in cold water. If you are using fresh pineapple, cook it first. Heat the crushed pineapple (do not drain) and stir in the softened gelatin until dissolved. Add the lemon juice and honey; chill until mixture is partially set. Then fold in the whipped cream, cheese, and nuts. Pour into molds and chill until set.

Grapefruit-Cream Cheese Mold

4 tbsp. gelatin
½ C. cold water
1 C. boiling water
1 C. honey, reserve 2 tbsp.
Fresh berries or
pomegranate seeds
1 C. chopped pecans

3 C. fresh pink grapefruit pieces
and juice (with all rind
and membrane removed)
8 oz. cream cheese
2 tbsp. light cream
¾ tsp. salt

Soften the gelatin in the cold water; add the boiling water and stir until gelatin is dissolved. Add honey, fresh berries or pomegranate seeds, and grapefruit. Pour half of this mixture into a 6-cup ring mold and refrigerate until set. Beat the cream cheese with the cream, 2 tbsp. honey, and salt. Stir in the nuts and spread over the set layer of gelatin. Pour the remaining gelatin into the mold and refrigerate until set.

Molded Chicken and Cucumber Salad

3 whole chicken breasts, split
(about 2¼ lbs.)
1 lg. onion, quartered
1 stalk celery with top, chopped
3 tsp. salt
6 whole peppercorns
3 C. water

4 tbsp. gelatin
¾ C. dry white wine
2 medium-sized cucumbers
¼ C. chopped green onion
1 tbsp. chopped fresh dill
1 C. mayonnaise
1 C. dairy sour cream

Combine chicken breasts, onion, celery, 2 tsp. of salt, peppercorns, and water in large saucepan. Bring to boiling; lower heat; simmer, covered, for 30 minutes or until chicken is tender. Remove from heat; cool in broth until cool enough to handle.

Lift chicken from broth; remove and discard skin and bones; dice meat; place in a large bowl. Strain stock into a measuring cup; there should be about 2 cups. If necessary, add water to make 2 cups. Return broth to saucepan; bring to boiling.

Sprinkle gelatin over ½ cup of the wine; let stand to soften 5 minutes. Stir into hot broth until dissolved. Measure out ¼ cup of the broth; combine with remaining ¼ cup wine and pour into an 8-cup mold. Place mold in a pan filled with ice and water; chill until mixture is syrupy-thick. Cut 15 to 18 thin slices from one cucumber; arrange overlapping on gelatin, pressing down slightly.

Shread remaining cucumber coarsely; you should have about 2 cups. Add to chicken along with onion and dill. Chill remaining gelatin mixture until syrupy-thick; stir in mayonnaise, sour cream, and the remaining 1 tsp. salt until smooth. Pour over chicken mixture; stir to mix. Carefully spoon into mold. Refrigerate several hours until firm. Unmold onto serving plate. Garnish.

Molded Cucumber Salad

1 cucumber, pared and diced	4 tsp. gelatin
½ tsp. salt	¼ C. cold water
½ sweet pimiento, diced	1 C. cream, whipped
½ tsp. lemon juice	

Combine cucumber, salt, pimiento, and lemon juice. Soak gelatin in cold water for 5 minutes; dissolve over hot water in a double boiler and mix thoroughly with whipped cream. Add cucumber mixture and pour into molds. Chill.

Tomato and Cheese Crown

4 tbsp. gelatin	1 stalk celery, chopped
½ C. cold water	1 tbsp. vinegar
2 C. diced fresh tomatoes	1 tbsp. onion juice
½ tsp. salt	½ tsp. pepper
1/16 tsp. pepper	1½ C. diced Swiss or
1 bay leaf	Monterey Jack cheese

Soften gelatin in cold water for 5 minutes. Cook tomatoes, add seasonings, bay leaf, and celery, and cook 10 minutes. Strain and add gelatin, vinegar, onion juice, and pepper, and stir until gelatin is dissolved. Add cheese, pour into mold, and chill until firm.

Chicory Crown Salad

8 oz. cream cheese	1 clove garlic, cut
½ tsp. salt	3 tbsp. gelatin
2 C. drained grated cucumber	¼ C. water
1 C. mayonnaise	1 head chicory
¼ C. minced onion	2 hard-cooked egg yolks, sieved
¼ C. minced parsley	

Mix first 6 ingredients in a bowl that has been rubbed with garlic. Soften gelatin in cold water and dissolve over hot water in a double boiler. Cool to lukewarm and combine with cheese mixture. Beat thoroughly and pack into a deep springform pan. Select chicory sprays of even height with perfect leaves. Stick whole sprays into the edge of the mixture close enough together to form a complete crown of greens. Chill until the mixture is firm. Remove from the mold onto a bed of chicory and sprinkle sieved egg yolks over top.

Cucumber Mousse

2 tsp. gelatin	¼ tsp. paprika
3 tbsp. cold water	1 C. pared, seeded,
2 tsp. vinegar or lemon juice	chopped cucumbers
1 tsp. grated onion	1 C. whipping cream, whipped
¾ tsp. salt	

Soak gelatin in cold water, then dissolve over heat. Add vinegar or lemon juice, onion, salt, and paprika. Chill until almost set. Beat the gelatin mixture gradually into the cream. Fold in the drained cucumbers. Fill individual molds with the mousse. When they are thoroughly chilled, invert the mousse onto a garnished platter.

Jellied Chicken or Veal Mousse

2 tbsp. gelatin	½ C. diced seeded cucumber
¾ C. chicken stock	Salt
3 egg yolks	Pepper
1½ C. milk	Paprika
2 C. minced cooked chicken or veal	1 C. whipping cream, whipped

Soak gelatin in ¼ C. chicken stock for 5 minutes. Dissolve in ½ C. hot stock. In top half of a double boiler, blend the beaten egg yolks and milk; add the dissolved gelatin. When mixture is cool, add cooked chicken or veal, diced cucumber, salt, pepper, and paprika. When syrupy fold in the whipped cream. Place the mousse in a wet mold and chill until firm.

Tomato Aspic

3½ C. chopped, peeled tomatoes	1 bay leaf
1 tsp. salt	4 stalks celery with leaves, chopped
½ tsp. paprika	1 tsp. dried basil or tarragon
3 tbsp. honey	3 tbsp. gelatin
2 tbsp. lemon juice	½ C. cold water
3 tbsp. chopped onion	

Simmer for 30 minutes, then strain, tomatoes, salt, paprika, honey, lemon juice, onion, bay leaf, celery, and basil or tarragon. Soak gelatin in cold water; dissolve it in the strained hot juice. Add water to make 4 cups of liquid. Chill the aspic. When it is about to set add 1 or 2 cups of solid ingredients, a choice or a combination of: sliced olives, chopped celery, chopped green peppers, grated or chopped carrots, chopped meat, flaked fish, or sliced avocados. Chill the aspic in mold until firm and serve.

Anchovy Dressing

4 tbsp. mashed anchovies	½ C. wine vinegar
1 C. olive oil	Dash or two black pepper

Shake vigorously for a minute or two and let stand, covered, in the refrigerator overnight.

Avocado Dressing

2 ripe avocados, peeled and mashed	3 tbsp. honey
Juice of ½ lemon	½ tsp. salt
	½ C. heavy cream

Blend together all ingredients except cream. Fold cream in finished dressing. Chill and serve the same day.

Bleu Cheese Dressing

2 C. sour cream	Dash of cayenne
2 C. crumbled bleu cheese	1 C. cream cheese
1 tsp. white pepper	1 tsp. tarragon vinegar

Blend above ingredients together in a mixer or blender until light and creamy smooth. To make a chunky dressing, add extra crumbled bleu cheese.

Celery Seed Dressing

2 C. olive oil	2 tsp. dry mustard
½ C. vinegar	2 tsp. paprika
2 tbsp. grated onion	4 tsp. celery seed

Combine all ingredients. Beat with rotary beater until well blended and thick. Chill several hours. Shake, and pour over your favorite salad.

Citrus Fruit Dressing

1 egg, beaten	2 tsp. grated lemon peel
¾ C. honey	1 C. yogurt
1 tbsp. grated orange peel	

Combine all ingredients except yogurt and cook over low heat, stirring continuously with wire whip until thick (about 5 minutes). Fold in yogurt. Chill.

Cottage Cheese Salad Dressing

1 C. large curd cottage cheese	4 tbsp. lemon juice
1 C. skim milk	½ C. chopped green pepper
2 tsp. salt	½ C. chopped green onions
½ tsp. black pepper	1 clove garlic, crushed

Whip ingredients together thoroughly.

Creamy Fruit Dressing

6 oz. cream cheese	½ tsp. salt
2 C. heavy cream	½ C. honey
2 tbsp. lemon juice	1 C. fresh strawberries

Place all ingredients in blender and blend well. Use this dressing on fresh fruit, fruit salad, or fresh fruit desserts. The color will be light pink. Yields 3 cups.

For variety in color and flavor, instead of strawberries, use fresh blueberries for a purple color, fresh peaches for an orange color, fresh apricots for a yellow color, fresh cherries for a deep rose color, pitted dates for a tan color, fresh grated coconut plus ½ C. coconut milk for a white color, or the juice of 1 fresh lime and 1 tsp. of the grated rind for a light green color. Add fresh chopped parsley to the grated rind for a dark green color. So natural, and will surprise your family and guests on a hot summer day.

Curried Yogurt Dressing

2 C. yogurt	1 tsp. salt
2 tbsp. dry mustard	1 tsp. cayenne
1 tbsp. prepared mustard	2 tsp. curry powder

Mix above ingredients with wire whip or blender until creamy smooth. Chill.

Fresh Mint Dressing

1 C. honey or dark cane syrup
½ C. lime juice

4 tbsp. chopped fresh mint leaves

In small bowl, stir all ingredients together until well blended.

Garlic Dressing

1 C. olive oil
1 C. red wine vinegar
4 cloves garlic, crushed
1 tsp. thyme

1 tsp. oregano
1 tsp. basil
2 bay leaves

Combine all ingredients in a jar and shake well. Let set at room temperature for 20 minutes, then refrigerate.

Green Goddess Dressing

1 recipe Blender Mayonnaise
4 anchovy fillets
1 tbsp. chopped scallion
3 tbsp. chopped parsley

1 tbsp. tarragon
2 tbsp. chopped chives
2 tbsp. cider vinegar

Blend at low speed until creamy and smooth.

Honey and Cream Dressing

4 C. sour cream
1 C. honey
1 lg. green pepper, chopped fine
4 tbsp. lemon juice
2 tsp. ground ginger

2 tsp. salt, optional
1 C. cider vinegar
1 tsp. dry mustard
2 C. safflower oil

Beat with a mixer until well blended.

Creamy Horseradish Dressing

2 C. sour cream
2 C. Blender Mayonnaise
½ C. hot horseradish

Dash or two
Worcestershire sauce

Stir all ingredients together until smooth. Add more horseradish if desired. This is very good for dunking raw vegetables.

Kelp Dressing

2 C. olive oil
Juice of 2 lemons

2 tbsp. powdered kelp

Shake the above ingredients together until well blended.

Lemon and Honey Dressing

1 C. honey

Juice of 2 lemons

Whirl in blender until creamy and fluffy.

Blender Mayonnaise

2 eggs
4 tbsp. cider vinegar
2 tsp. honey
2 tsp. dry mustard

1 tsp. salt
Dash or two white pepper
1 C. olive oil

Blend at low speed all ingredients except ¾ cup of oil for 1 minute. Then remove the center cover of the blender and slowly pour in the rest of the oil, blending until very well mixed.

Cooked Mayonnaise

4 tbsp. all-purpose flour	4 eggs
6 tbsp. honey	2 C. water
2 tsp. salt	½ C. cider vinegar
1 tsp. dry mustard	6 tbsp. safflower or
Dash or 2 cayenne	vegetable oil

In a medium saucepan mix flour, honey, salt, mustard, and cayenne. In bowl beat eggs and 2 cups of water with wire whisk; add vinegar, then flour mixture a little at a time until smooth. Add lemon juice a little at a time. Cook in a double boiler, stirring constantly until thick. Remove from heat and stir in oil. Cover and refrigerate until well chilled.

Coleslaw Dressing

Prepare Cooked Mayonnaise, increasing dry mustard to 3 tsp.

Louis Sauce

1 C. Cooked Mayonnaise	½ C. catsup
1 tbsp. vinegar	

Combine all ingredients and mix well.

Oil and Vinegar Dressing with Herbs

½ C. oil	1 tsp. garlic salt
1 C. vinegar	1 tsp. chopped parsley
1 tsp. basil	1 tsp. thyme
1 tsp. onion juice	

Shake all ingredients together, and let stand overnight.

Sesame-Tomato Dressing

3 C. sesame seeds
1 C. olive oil
½ C. honey
½ onion, chopped

Juice of 2 lemons
2 fresh tomatoes, skins removed
2 cloves garlic, minced

To remove the tomato skins quickly and easily, dip each tomato in boiling water. Sauté garlic and sesame seed in oil until slightly brown. Blend all ingredients in electric blender for 1 minute.

Sour Cream Dressing

3 C. sour cream
1 C. cooked mayonnaise
2 tbsp. lemon juice
2 tbsp. honey

½ tsp. salt
Dash or two paprika
Dash of cayenne

Blend above ingredients together, covering when you refrigerate because it picks up odors very quickly.

Tomato Dressing

6 fresh red tomatoes,
   skins removed
3 tbsp. cider vinegar
4 tbsp. honey

1 sm. onion, minced
½ tsp. minced dill
½ tsp. basil

To remove the tomato skins quickly and easily, dip each tomato in boiling water. Blend ingredients together in blender until tomatoes are liquified. This dressing is very good on spinach salad. For added zest add a little red wine. Garnish top with chopped eggs.

Garnishes

Apple Cups: Cut the top from an apple that stands up straight. Remove pulp from the apple, leaving a quarter-inch-thick shell. With a small pointed knife, mark petal shapes. Cut along marking. Be sure to brush surface of apple with lemon juice to keep it from darkening.

Bread Crumbs: Toast stale bread, crumble or grate, and sprinkle in soup or on casserole.

Carrot Curls: Shave carrots lengthwise with a vegetable parer in long strips. Roll around finger and place in ice water. They keep very well.

Carrots: Shred or grate and sprinkle over soups or other dishes.

Cauliflowerets: Remove outside greens and break each floweret apart. Chill.

Celery Curls: Cut celery stalks into 3-inch pieces with a sharp knife. Beginning at the outer edge, make 4 to 6 parallel cuts, extending about a third of the way down the stalk. Put in ice water and they will curl.

Celery Sticks: Cut each celery stalk in half and cut in thin strips. Placed in ice water, these keep well.

Cinnamon Sticks: Great in teas and punches; also may be chewed to sweeten the breath.

Cucumber Balls: Cut large cucumbers into balls with a melon baller and marinate in herb dressing.

Cucumber Boats: Cut cukes in half lengthwise and scoop out pulp. Fill with your favorite filling or salad.

Cucumber Tulips: Cut the ends from unpeeled cukes. Cut into 2-inch lengths. Cut 6 triangle sections down from cut edge, making petals. Scoop out remaining seeds. Place a small rounded bit of carrot or beet on a toothpick and press in center. Chill in ice water so petal will open more.

Cucumber Twist: Cut cukes in thin slices. Cut each slice once from edges in opposite directions so slice will stand up slightly.

Egg Trick: Slice, quarter, or grate hard-boiled eggs to use as garnish.

Gelatin Balls: Leftover gelatin makes perfect balls for garnishing salads. Dip melon baller in hot water before each scoop.

Grated Cheese: Crumble over salad or open-face sandwiches.

Green Peas in Pod: Served with vegetable dips; guests shell their own or eat pod with dips.

Green Pepper Rings: Cut crosswise slices from peppers and remove membranes and seeds.

Ice Cream Mold: Press ice cream into small fruit-shaped molds and freeze until firm. Remove from molds and add stem to look like a strawberry, lemon, or banana. Use florist leaves, frilled toothpicks.

Lemon Flowers: With a sharp knife slice lemon skin only ¾ of the way down in 8 to 10 wedges. Spread the skin from the fruit and tuck the end next to the skin. Place among greens.

Lemon, Orange, or Lime Wheels: Slice fruit thinly. Cut U-shaped notches in peel only.

Onion Chrysanthemums: Peel a uniformly shaped onion. Cut a thin slice from the top. Cut vertically into quarters to within a half inch of the bottom. Force toothpicks into the bottom of each cut. Put the onion upside down in enough cold water to cover. The onion can be colored with beet juice or any other natural coloring. Allow to stand in refrigerator for 24 hours, during which time the layers of onion will separate to form "petals." Remove and drain on a paper towel.

Parmesan: Grate over salads or meat dishes.

Parsley: Chop and sprinkle over soup, casseroles, or serve in sprigs with salads.

Pickle Fans: Use small sweet or dill pickles. Starting at the tip, cut thin slices almost to the stem. Spread slices to form fans.

Pomegranate Seeds: Crush to make food coloring.

Radishes: Slice thin and sprinkle over salads and molds.

Radish Accordions: Start at the top and cut thin slices ¾ way through until you get to the bottom. Place in cold water. Will keep 2 or 3 days.

Radish Roses: Cut 4 or 5 thin vertical slices around radish and place in ice water and radish will open. May be stored, covered, in the refrigerator for 2 to 3 days.

Seasoned Croutons: Fry whole wheat cubes in peanut oil until golden. Drain well. Season with a mixture of cayenne, Parmesan cheese, paprika, and sesame seeds; sprinkle over croutons, and stir slightly.

Soy Bean Bits: Soak, grate, and toast soy beans, and use in place of bread crumbs.

Strawberry Fans: Choose firm berries. Leaving hulls on, cut in thin slices from tip almost to the stem. Spread slices to form a fan.

Tinted Coconut: For red, place the juice of one fresh, bright red strawberry in a jar with coconut. Close, and shake; for green, use ½ tsp. of fresh parsley juice.

Toasted Almonds: Spread shelled almonds on cookie sheet and bake at 350°. Turn every few minutes until roasted.

Toasted Sesame Seeds: Broil, turning until golden. Pumpkin, sunflower, and squash seeds may be toasted in the same manner.

Tomato Peel Rose: With a sharp knife cut a continuous strip of peel from a tomato. Roll tightly, but gently, skin side out; hold the end in place with a toothpick. If you want two smaller roses, cut peel in half.

Vegetable cutouts: Cut peeled turnips, carrots, kohlrabi, or rutabaga into thin crosswise slices. Cut with canapé cutters, either round or scalloped. Flower shapes are made from evenly cut U-shaped notches around the circle of the vegetable. To form rounded petals, cut off corners. Cut very thin slices and watch the flowers bloom.

Watercress: A sprig or two of watercress with sliced, stuffed olives makes a beautiful flower bouquet for molds and aspic.

Zucchini Slices: Score with fork from end to end, then slice thinly.

Breads

Good homemade bread is easy to make, and it's fun. When made with whole wheat flour (a small grinder is a good investment), it is among the most nutritious of foods, because it is eaten so regularly and in such generous quantities.

I believe the public has been misled into believing that fortified breads are just as nutritious as the unrefined products. But many vitamins and minerals, the most important of all being the valuable protein in the germ of wheat, are removed during refining. I have been told that many millers find it a very expensive process stirring the iron and vitamins into their white flours, so they omit it and still call their breads enriched. So why do they continue to sell these devitalized products?

Not only do breads of unrefined flours contribute iron, vitamin E, many B vitamins, and valuable protein, they can be made more health-producing by additions of valuable foods such as non-fat milk, wheat germ, and soy or rice flours. Fresh wheat germ is the most nutritious part of the grain and should be used freely.

Every home should know the fragrant odor and delicious flavor of homemade bread. And we all have the right to discover that bread-making can be a most rewarding hobby. Individuals who think it impossible to make delicious breads of whole grain flours should remember that our great-grandmothers, who took pride in their baking, used only whole grain flours because no other was available.

Basic Bread

The breadmaking technique is simple and straightforward. Here are the basic steps. The ingredients and proportions vary from recipe to recipe. In these recipes don't sift flour; use only Royal baking powder, which contains no aluminum. (See page 23 for recipe).

1. Pour water into a bowl, add yeast and a little honey, and let stand until the yeast rises to the top. Water should be 72° to 80°.
2. Add oil, molasses, and honey; stir until well blended.
3. Add flour by the cupful, beating until smooth and elastic, resting when you get tired.
4. Add more flour until dough is no longer sticky.
5. Turn out on a board, and begin the kneading process, adding a little flour if the dough begins to get sticky.
6. Kneading is finished when dough is not sticky, but smooth and satiny.
7. Place dough in a greased bowl, turn once. Cover bowl with plastic wrap to keep out air and place in a warm place (80°) to rise.
8. Allow dough to rise until doubled, about 1 hour.
9. Make an indentation with a couple of fingers. If the indentation remains, the dough is ready to be shaped into loaves or rolls.
10. Place the shaped bread in greased and floured pans, cover, and allow to rise for 45 minutes in a warm place (80°).
11. Bake in 350° preheated oven for about 45 minutes to 1 hour. The test for doneness is quite simple: when bread begins to leave sides of pan and is golden brown, it's ready.

Basic Whole Wheat Bread

4 C. warm water	½ C. honey
½ C. peanut oil	¼ C. molasses
2 tsp. salt	8 to 10 C. fresh whole wheat flour
1½ pkg. dry yeast, dissolved in ¼ C. warm water	

Follow Basic Bread steps for mixing and baking. This recipe yields 3 loaves.

Rye Bread

Follow Basic Whole Wheat recipe using 6-7 C. rye flour and 2-3 C. whole wheat flour mixed together. Follow Basic Bread steps for mixing and baking. This bread will not be golden brown, but dark and crusty. Brush with melted butter for a more tender crust.

Onion Bread

Follow Basic Whole Wheat recipe. Omit molasses and add 1½ C. minced onions. Shape into round balls and place on a greased cookie sheet about 4 or 5 inches apart. Bake at 350° for 45 to 60 minutes. Brush with melted butter.

Poppy Seed Loaf

Follow Basic Whole Wheat recipe. Instead of forming in loaves to bake, pinch off pieces about 2 inches in diameter and roll in hands, making balls. Drop each ball in melted butter and roll in poppy seeds. Pile the balls two layers deep into slightly greased loaf pans. Allow to rise until almost double. Bake at 350° for about 1 hour.

Light Rye Bread

Follow Basic Whole Wheat recipe using a mixture of 6 - 7 C. rye flour and 2 - 3 C. unbleached flour.

Oatmeal Bread

Follow Basic Whole Wheat recipe. Use 2 C. of oat flour in place of 2 C. of whole wheat flour. Oat flour can be made at home by whirling steel cut oats or rolled oats in an electric blender until very fine. Bake at 350° for 50 minutes. Brush with butter.

Pumpernickel Bread

Follow Basic Whole Wheat recipe. Add 3 tbsp. of caraway seeds with liquids. Use 2 C. bran flour, 3 C. rye flour, and 3 to 5 C. whole wheat flour. Bran flour can be made by whirling bran cereal in your blender until very fine. Bake at 375° for 50 minutes. Brush with butter.

Soy Bean Bread

Follow basic recipe for Whole Wheat Bread. The night before, rinse 2 C. soy beans and soak in water to cover. Save water and use as part of water in recipe. Grind soy beans in blender until fine and mushy. Add soy bean mush with liquids. Use 3 C. graham flour in place of 3 C. of whole wheat flour. Use a greased glass casserole dish to bake this bread at 350° for 1 hour. Brush top with butter.

Amahl Bread

2 C. water	1 C. warm water (90° to 100°)
½ C. yellow cornmeal	2 pkg. active dry yeast
¼ C. butter	7½ C. unsifted whole wheat flour
½ C. light molasses	2 tbsp. melted butter
1 tbsp. salt	

In medium saucepan, bring 2 C. water to boil; gradually stir in ½ C. cornmeal, mixing until smooth. Cook, stirring until thick, about 1 minute. Remove from heat. Add butter, molasses, and salt. Stir until butter melts. Set aside; let cool to lukewarm. If possible, check temperature of warm water in a large mixing bowl before adding yeast. Stir until dissolved.

To yeast add molasses mixture and 3 C. flour; beat until smooth, about 2 minutes. Gradually add rest of flour; mix in by hand until the dough leaves sides of bowl.

Turn dough onto lightly floured pastry cloth. Dough will be stiff. Knead until smooth (about 10 minutes).

Place in lightly greased large bowl; turn to bring up greased side. Cover with towel; let rise in warm place until double in bulk, about 1 hour.

Lightly grease and flour two loaf pans. Turn out dough onto lightly floured pastry cloth. Divide in half. Roll out one half into 12-by-8-inch rectangle; roll up, starting at one end. Press ends even; pinch to seal; tuck under loaf.

Place seam side down in prepared loaf pan. Brush surface of loaf lightly with the melted butter; sprinkle with a little yellow cornmeal. Repeat with other half of dough. Preheat oven to 375°. Let loaves rise in warm place until sides come to top of pans and tops are rounded, 1 hour. Set oven rack at middle level. Bake 50 to 55 minutes, or until crust is deep golden-brown and loaves sound hollow when tapped with knuckle. Turn out of pans and let loaves cool completely.

French Bread

This bread also makes a wonderful pizza crust.

2 tbsp. yeast	7 to 8 C. unbleached white flour
½ C. warm water	1 egg white mixed with
1 tbsp. salt	1 tbsp. water
2 C. lukewarm water (76° to 82°)	

Soften the yeast in ½ C. warm water. Combine the salt and 2 C. lukewarm water; beat in 2 C. of flour. Blend in the softened yeast; stir in 4 to 5 C. of flour, making a soft dough. Turn out and knead 10 minutes. Cover and let the dough rest for 5 minutes. Knead again, working in the rest of the flour until dough is smooth.

Let rise in a greased bowl, in a warm place, until double. Punch down and form in loaf or desired shape. Sprinkle cornmeal on bottom of greased pan or cookie sheet before you place bread in it; brush with egg white. Let rise, and bake at 350°.

Applesauce Bread

2 C. applesauce	2 tsp. salt
2 eggs, slightly beaten	1 tsp. baking soda
½ C. melted butter	1 tsp. cinnamon
1 C. honey	2 tsp. nutmeg
½ C. brown sugar	1 C. seedless raisins
4 C. whole wheat flour	2 C. coarsely chopped pecans
2 tbsp. Royal baking powder	

Combine the applesauce, eggs, butter, honey, and brown sugar. Blend well. Stir in the flour, baking powder, salt, soda, and spices. Stir this mixture until smooth. Add raisins and chopped nuts. Stir 8 to 10 times. Turn batter into 2 greased and floured loaf pans. Bake at 350° for 1 hour. Cool before slicing.

Honey Pineapple Bread

2 tbsp. corn oil
1 C. honey
1 egg, slightly beaten
2 C. whole wheat flour
2 tsp. Royal baking powder

¾ tsp. salt
1 C. whole bran
1 C. pineapple juice
¾ C. chopped walnuts

In a bowl blend thoroughly the oil, honey, and egg. Stir in the flour, baking powder, salt, whole bran, and pineapple juice, mixing just until dry ingredients are moistened. Fold in the nuts. Pour batter into a greased and floured loaf pan and bake at 350° for 1 hour.

Oatmeal Applesauce Loaf

4 tart apples, peeled,
  cored, and sliced
⅓ C. water
2 C. brown sugar, firmly packed
2 eggs
1½ C. whole wheat flour
1 tsp. Royal baking powder
1 tsp. soda

1½ tsp. salt
1 tsp. cinnamon
½ tsp. nutmeg
⅓ C. melted butter
1½ C. rolled oats
½ C. coarsely chopped walnuts
1 C. raisins

In a covered saucepan, simmer apples in water for 15 minutes, or until tender, then add 1 C. brown sugar and continue cooking until sugar dissolves. Mash apples with potato masher until smooth; cool. Beat together remaining brown sugar and eggs until smooth; add 1 C. of the applesauce. Stir flour with baking powder, soda, salt, cinnamon, and nutmeg into egg mixture; blend thoroughly. Stir in melted butter, rolled oats, raisins, and nuts. Spoon batter into a well-greased and floured loaf pan. Bake at 350° for 1 hour.

Barley Flour Muffins

2 C. barley flour
2 tsp. Royal baking powder
½ tsp. salt
¼ C. honey or molasses

2 C. milk or water
¼ C. oil
¼ tsp. vanilla extract

Combine dry ingredients. Combine wet ingredients. Fold dry and wet ingredients together, just until all the flour is moistened. Spoon into oiled muffin tin. Bake 20 minutes at 400°.

Bran Muffins I

1 C. bran flour	¼ C. peanut oil
1 C. whole wheat flour	½ C. honey
2 tsp. Royal baking powder	1½ C. milk
½ tsp. salt	¼ C. molasses
1 egg, beaten	

Combine dry ingredients. Combine wet ingredients. Quickly fold wet and dry together, just until flour is moistened. Spoon into greased muffin tin. Bake at 400° for about 20 minutes.

Bran Muffins II

⅛ C. honey	1 egg, beaten
1 C. soft butter	½ C. whole wheat flour
1 tsp. soda	2 C. bran flour
1 C. buttermilk	½ C. raisins

Cream honey and butter. Dissolve soda in buttermilk and add to honey and butter. Stir in rest of ingredients. Bake in greased muffin tin at 400° for 20 minutes. Let stand 5 minutes before removing. These are light and delicious muffins.

Bran Muffins III

1 C. buttermilk	⅓ C. butter
2 C. shredded whole bran	⅓ C. dark brown sugar, packed
1 C. whole wheat flour	1 egg
1 tsp. Royal baking powder	3 tbsp. dark molasses
½ tsp. soda	⅓ C. plumped raisins
½ tsp. salt	

Preheat oven to 400°. Measure buttermilk into a bowl. Stir in bran and let stand a few minutes. Stir flour to lighten, measure, add dry ingredients, and stir again. Beat butter and sugar until creamy, using rotary beater. Add egg, beat until smooth and fluffy. Beat in molasses. Clean off beater, using wooden spoon. Add flour and bran mixture alternately in 3 portions, beating until smooth after each addition. Fold in raisins. Spoon into greased muffin pan. Bake 20 minutes or until golden brown. Serve hot.

Whole Wheat Muffins

2 C. whole wheat flour	¼ C. peanut oil
2 tsp. Royal baking powder	½ C. honey
½ tsp. salt	1½ C. milk
1 egg, beaten	

Combine dry ingredients. Combine wet ingredients. Quickly fold wet and dry together, just until flour is moistened. Spoon into greased muffin tin. Bake at 400° for about 20 minutes.

Corn Meal Muffins

2 C. cornmeal	¼ C. corn oil
2 tsp. Royal baking powder	½ C. honey
½ tsp. salt	1½ C. milk
1 egg, beaten	

Combine dry ingredients. Combine wet ingredients. Quickly fold wet and dry together, just until meal is moistened. Spoon into greased muffin tin. Bake at 400° for about 20 minutes.

Rice Muffins

1 C. whole wheat flour	1 egg
1 tbsp. raw sugar	⅔ C. milk
½ tsp. salt	1 C. cold cooked brown rice
1½ tsp. Royal baking powder	4 tbsp. melted butter

Stir flour to lighten, then stir in sugar, salt, and baking powder. Beat egg thoroughly, add milk and rice; stir in butter immediately, add the flour mixture, and stir until dry ingredients are just dampened; then stir 3 or 4 more times, but not until smooth. Spoon quickly into buttered muffin pans, filling ⅔ full. Bake at 425° for 20 minutes or until nicely browned. Serve hot.

Spice Muffins

2 C. whole wheat flour	¼ tsp. ground allspice
2 tsp. Royal baking powder	¼ tsp. grated ginger
½ tsp. salt	1 egg, beaten
½ tsp. cinnamon	¼ C. corn oil
½ tsp. powdered mace	½ C. honey
¼ tsp. nutmeg	1½ C. milk

Combine dry ingredients. Quickly fold wet and dry together, just until flour is moistened. Spoon into greased muffin tin. Bake at 400° for about 20 minutes.

Buckwheat Muffins

2 C. buckwheat flour	¼ C. honey
1 tbsp. cinnamon	3 C. water
1 tsp. salt	A sprinkle of toasted
1½ tsp. Royal baking powder	sesame seeds

Mix dry ingredients except sesame seeds. Combine honey and water and add to dry ingredients gradually, mixing thoroughly to make smooth batter. Ladle into oiled muffin tins, filling half way. Sprinkle on sesame seeds. Bake 30-40 minutes at 400°. Muffins are crispy outside, soft inside.

Date-Nut Loaf

¾ C. boiling water	¼ tsp. salt
½ lb. pitted dates, finely cut	1 tsp. soda
2 tbsp. butter	2 eggs, well beaten
½ C. honey	1 C. shredded Cheddar cheese
1¾ C. whole wheat flour	1 C. chopped walnuts

Pour boiling water over the dates and butter; add honey. Let stand about 5 minutes, until all the butter is melted and the mixture has cooled. Stir flour with the salt and soda, into a bowl. Stir in the date-honey mixture, beaten eggs, cheese, and walnuts. Stir only until well blended. Pour into a well-buttered and floured loaf pan. Bake at 325° for 50 to 60 minutes. Turn out on a rack to cool.

Herb Corn Sticks

1⅔ C. whole wheat flour	½ tsp. thyme
3 tsp. Royal baking powder	1 egg
½ tsp. salt	3 tbsp. honey
¾ C. corn meal	1½ C. milk
½ tsp. dried marjoram flakes	¼ C. melted butter

Stir together flour, baking powder, and salt. Stir in corn meal, marjoram, and thyme. In another bowl beat egg and honey. Stir in milk and melted butter, then add all at once to the dry ingredients. Stir just until mixture is moistened. Spoon into well-greased corn stick pans, filling about ¾ full. Bake in a 425° oven for 20 minutes, or until golden brown.

Fresh Fruit Loaf

1 C. brown sugar, firmly packed	1 C. pitted fresh dates, cut in small pieces
½ C. peanut oil	
2 tbsp. sherry (optional)	2 tsp. soda
1 tsp. vanilla	2 C. whole wheat flour
1 C. raisins	½ tsp. salt
1 C. coarsely cut mixed fruit	¼ tsp. cinnamon
1 C. chopped nuts	¼ tsp. nutmeg

In a large mixing bowl, mix together brown sugar, oil, sherry, and vanilla. Mix raisins, fruits, nuts, and dates with the soda; stir into sugar mixture. Combine flour with salt, cinnamon, and nutmeg; add to sugar-fruit mix. Stir to blend thoroughly. Turn into a greased and floured loaf pan and bake at 350° for 1 hour, 25 minutes; turn onto wire rack to cool.

Apricot Nut Bread

1 C. dried apricots	2 tsp. Royal baking powder
2 C. water	1 tsp. soda
1 C. honey	1 tsp. salt
2 tbsp. butter	½ C. non-fat dry milk
1 egg	¾ C. apricot liquid
Peel of 1 orange, grated	½ C. orange juice
3½ C. whole wheat flour	¼ C. chopped walnuts

Cover the apricots with the water and simmer until apricots are tender but not mushy; drain off liquid and save. Cream together honey and butter; beat in egg and grated orange peel. Stir flour with baking powder, soda, and salt. Add milk and stir. Add to creamed mixture alternately with apricot and orange juices. Chop apricots and stir into batter with the walnut meats. Spoon into two greased and floured loaf pans. Bake at 350° for 40 to 45 minutes, or until bread springs back when touched in the center.

Carrot Bread

4 eggs	1½ tsp. soda
2 C. honey	¼ tsp. salt
1½ C. corn oil	2 tsp. cinnamon
3 C. whole wheat flour	2 C. finely shredded raw carrots
2 tsp. Royal baking powder	

Beat the eggs and add the honey gradually, beating until thick. Add the oil gradually and continue beating until thoroughly combined. Stir in the flour, baking powder, soda, salt, and cinnamon until mixture is smooth. Stir in the carrots until blended well. Turn into 1 large or 2 small greased loaf pans, filling them no more than ⅔ full. Bake the bread at 350° for 1 hour for a large loaf, or 45 minutes for small loaves.

Carrot-Coconut Bread

3 eggs	1 C. chopped walnuts
½ C. unrefined soy oil	2 C. whole wheat flour
1 tsp. vanilla	½ tsp. salt
2 C. finely shredded carrots	1 tsp. soda
2 C. grated coconut	1 tsp. Royal baking powder
1 C. honey	1 tsp. cinnamon
1 C. raisins	

In a large bowl, beat the eggs until light. Stir in oil and vanilla; add carrots, coconut, honey, raisins, and nuts, and mix until well blended. Combine the flour, salt, soda, baking powder, and cinnamon. Stir into egg mixture just until well blended. Spoon into a loaf pan that has been well buttered and dusted with flour. Bake at 350° for about 1 hour. Remove from pan and cool thoroughly. Its flavor and texture improve if wrapped and refrigerated for several days.

Orange or Tangerine Nut Bread

¾ C. orange peel (pared from 3 large oranges with potato peeler)	1 egg, beaten
	1 C. finely chopped walnuts
	1 C. milk
1 C. water	4 C. whole wheat flour
1 C. honey	3 tsp. Royal baking powder
1 C. brown sugar, firmly packed	½ tsp. salt
1 tbsp. butter	

Put orange peel and water into electric blender, and whirl at high speed until peel is cut into fine pieces (or put peel through food chopper with finest blade three times, or until peel is fine, then combine with water. Put the orange-water mixture and the honey into a pan and bring to a boil, stirring until reduced to 1 C. (about 15 minutes). Set aside. In a bowl, combine the brown sugar and butter with a fork until butter is like coarse crumbs. Stir in the egg, walnuts, and orange peel mixture with the milk, mixing just until combined. Combine dry ingredients. Turn into a well-buttered and floured loaf pan, and bake in a 350° oven for 45 minutes for 2 small loaves or 1 hour for a large loaf. Cool and slice.

Cranberry-Orange Bread

1 C. honey	1 tsp. soda
3 tbsp. butter	1 tsp. salt
1 egg	1 lb. can whole cranberry sauce
Grated peel of 1 large orange	Juice of 1 large orange
3 C. whole wheat flour	1 C. broken walnuts
2 tsp. Royal baking powder	½ C. wheat germ

Combine together thoroughly the honey and butter, and beat in the egg; blend in orange peel. Blend flour with baking powder, soda, and salt; set aside. Drain cranberries. Reserving cranberries, add orange juice to the cranberry syrup. Add this juice combination alternately with the dry ingredients to the creamed mixture, blending after each addition. Stir in cranberries, walnuts, and wheat germ. Turn into a large, greased and floured loaf pan; bake at 350° for about 60 minutes. Cool before slicing.

Whole Wheat Banana Bread

4 oz. butter or margarine	½ tsp. salt
1 C. brown sugar	1 tsp. soda
2 eggs, slightly beaten	2 C. whole wheat flour
1 C. mashed bananas,	⅓ C. hot water
3 medium-sized bananas	½ C. chopped walnuts

Melt butter and blend in sugar. Mix in beaten eggs and mashed bananas, blending until smooth. Combine salt, soda, and whole wheat flour. Add dry ingredients alternately with hot water. Stir in chopped nut meats. Turn into a greased loaf pan and bake at 325° for one hour and 10 minutes.

Cheese Logs

¼ lb. soft butter	¼ tsp. curry powder (optional)
2 tsp. hot water	1 egg, beaten
1½ C. whole wheat flour	Sesame or poppy seeds
½ C. shredded sharp	
Cheddar cheese	

In small bowl with electric mixer, whip butter on medium speed for 2 minutes, adding hot water gradually. Add flour, mixing to make soft dough. Stir in cheese and curry powder. Chill until stiff enough to handle. On floured board, roll dough into logs ½ inch in diameter; cut into 2 inch pieces. Brush with beaten egg, roll in sesame seeds or poppy seeds, and place 1 inch apart on greased baking sheet. Bake at 375° for 12 minutes or until firm.

Whole Wheat Biscuits

1 C. whole wheat flour	2¼ tsp. Royal baking powder
1 C. unbleached flour	⅓ C. butter
¾ tsp. salt	¾ C. milk

Stir whole wheat flour, unbleached flour, salt, and baking powder together; cut in butter with a pastry blender. Add milk all at once and stir vigorously until dough just stiffens up, then turn out onto a lightly floured board and knead 6 times. Roll or pat out to thickness of ½ inch, and cut out with a biscuit cutter. Place on greased baking sheet. Bake in a 450° oven about 12 minutes.

Boston Brown Bread

1 C. cornmeal	1 tsp. salt
1 C. whole rye flour	¾ C. molasses
1 C. whole wheat flour	2 C. buttermilk
1 tsp. soda	½ C. seedless raisins

Mix cornmeal and flours, soda, and salt in a large bowl. Stir well. Combine molasses and buttermilk, add to the dry ingredients, stir until dry ingredients are just damp, then beat hard for a minute. With the last few stirs, add the washed and dried raisins. Pour batter into well-buttered molds or cans, filling them ⅔ full. Put on lids. Steam for 50 to 60 minutes, or until springy when pressed and no longer sticky. To improvise a steamer, set a rack in the bottom of a deep kettle, cover the bottom with boiling water, and place molds on the rack; cover kettle tightly. Replenish water as it boils away. Cool in the molds for a few minutes, then turn out and serve warm.

Spoon Corn Bread

2¼ C. milk
2 tbsp. butter
1 tsp. salt

⅔ C. corn meal
3 eggs, separated

Heat milk to scalding; add butter and salt and slowly stir in corn meal. Cook for 1 minute, stirring constantly. Remove from heat and cool a few minutes; then stir into well-beaten egg yolks. Fold in stiffly beaten egg whites and pour into a 4-cup casserole. Bake at 375° for 35 to 40 minutes. Serve from baking dish, with plenty of butter.

Peanut Bread

1¾ C. whole wheat flour
1 tsp. soda
½ tsp. salt
1 C. honey

½ C. peanut butter
1 egg, well-beaten
1 C. buttermilk

Stir flour; combine with soda and salt. Blend honey into peanut butter. Stir in well-beaten egg and beat until smooth. Add flour mixture and buttermilk alternately, beating until smooth after each addition. Turn into buttered loaf pan and bake at 350° for 1 hour or until well browned.

Granola Bread

½ C. corn oil
½ C. honey
2 eggs
1 C. granola

1 tbsp. Royal baking powder
2 C. whole wheat flour
½ C. milk

Mix oil, honey, and eggs together. Mix all dry ingredients together. Alternately, add the flour mixture and milk to oil mixture, stirring constantly. Bake in greased and floured mold or loaf pan at 350° for 1 hour.

Lemon Bread

½ C. peanut oil
1 C. honey
2 eggs
2 C. whole wheat flour
1 tbsp. Royal baking powder
½ tsp. salt

½ C. milk
½ C. chopped walnuts
Grated peel of 1 lemon
2 tbsp. honey
Juice of 1 lemon

Mix oil, honey, and eggs. Mix together all dry ingredients except nuts. Alternately add the flour mixture and the milk to the oil mixture, stirring constantly. Mix the nuts and lemon peel. Bake in greased and floured mold or loaf pan at 350° for 1 hour. Poke holes in warm cake with skewer, combine 2 tbsp. of honey with the juice of 1 lemon, and pour over top.

Whole Wheat Seed Pancakes

1½ C. whole wheat flour
1 tbsp. baking powder
½ tsp. salt
¾ C. sesame seeds
¼ C. slightly toasted
    sunflower seeds

1½ C. milk or buttermilk
1 or 2 eggs
3 tbsp. honey

Stir together dry ingredients. Mix wet ingredients. Combine dry and wet just enough to moisten. Cook in a medium griddle with a little bit of butter.

Granola

7 C. rolled oats
2 C. raw wheat germ
1 to 2 C. sesame seeds
2 C. shredded coconut
1 tsp. salt

1 C. sunflower seeds
½ C. boiled water
1 C. honey
¾ C. peanut oil

Mix together all dry ingredients. Dissolve honey in boiled water and combine oil with it. Pour the wet ingredients into the dry ones and give them a good mixing. Bake in oven at 250°, turning until golden brown. For an even tastier treat, add almonds, cashews, pecans, or anything your heart desires.

Scripture Bread

4 C. I Kings 5:11
½ C. I Samuel 14:25
½ C. Genesis 24:17
2 Isaiah 10:14

1 C. Judges 5:25
1 tsp. Leviticus 2:13
½ C. Isaiah 7:22 (melted)

Follow Samuel's instructions to the cook, I Samuel 9:23-24. Bake at 350° in a well-oiled shallow pan. This is a very earthy bread.

Basic Buttermilk Pancakes

2 C. unbleached white flour
1 tsp. Royal baking powder
½ tsp. salt
1½ C. buttermilk

½ C. honey
½ C. sour cream
2 eggs
½ C. melted butter

Stir dry ingredients together. Beat all wet ingredients with eggs. Add dry ingredients a little at a time to egg mixture, until smooth. Be sure not to overbeat. For each pancake pour about ¼ cup of batter on a lightly buttered hot griddle or skillet and cook until top is covered with bubbles and bottom is golden. Turn and cook until bottom is golden. Serve hot with natural maple syrup or honey.

Add to pancake batter any of the following variations:
1. ¾ C. fresh or drained blueberries
2. ¾ C. wheat germ plus ½ C. additional liquid
3. ¾ C. chopped dried dates, figs, or peaches
4. ½ C. carob powder plus ¼ C. additional liquid
5. ½ C. grated fresh coconut plus ¼ C. additional liquid
6. ¾ C. granola plus ½ C. additional liquid (these will be crunchy)
7. ½ C. chopped pecans plus 2 eggs plus ¼ C. water
8. Indian Harvest: ¾ C. cut sweet fresh corn
9. ½ C. brewers yeast plus ¼ C. additional liquid

Basic Buckwheat Pancakes

2 C. buckwheat flour	½ tsp. salt
1 C. unbleached white flour	½ C. melted butter
1 tsp. Royal baking powder	1¾ C. water
½ C. raw sugar	2 eggs, beaten
1 C. non-fat dry milk	

Stir all dry ingredients together. Beat all wet ingredients with eggs. Add dry ingredients a little at a time to egg mixture, beating 5 or 6 strokes until a little thicker than molasses. Cook in the same manner as Basic Buttermilk pancakes. Any of the variations may be adapted to this recipe as well.

Buckwheat Waffles

1¾ C. buckwheat flour	3 eggs
1 tsp. Royal baking powder	½ C. corn oil
½ tsp. salt (sea salt)	1½ C. non-fat milk
2 tsp. raw sugar	

Heat waffle iron according to manufacturer's directions. Stir dry ingredients with the wire whip. Beat eggs well in large bowl. Add corn oil and milk to the dry ingredients. Blend well. Pour batter into waffle iron, close, and bake until steaming stops.

Corn Fritters Supreme

1 C. whole wheat flour	Dash pepper
1½ tsp. Royal baking powder	2 eggs
¼ tsp. salt	¾ C. non-fat milk
½ tsp. ground cinnamon	1½ C. corn cut fresh from cob

Mix dry ingredients except corn together with wire whip. Mix eggs and milk together. Combine wet and dry ingredients until moistened. Fold in corn and stir together. Cook as you would any pancake. These will be light and fluffy. Serve with honey if you like, or in the place of bread.

Main Dishes

In this section are vegetable, rice, egg, poultry, fish, and meat dishes. All are treated as main dishes rather than side dishes since most of them could serve as the center of a breakfast, luncheon, or supper menu. The ingredients of casseroles and combinations follow Edgar Cayce's recommendations for eighty percent alkaline ash to twenty percent acid ash in the diet.

VEGETABLES

The philosophical as well as practical advantages of your own vegetable garden should be given serious consideration. So you smile to yourself as you read that statement, wondering what the person living in the metropolitan high rise can do. When fresh produce is unavailable, frozen vegetables can be substituted. The "Cayce" philosophy behind this is that frozen vegetables are normally grown and picked near the factory where they are quick frozen, thus allowing more maturity and not having to be picked very far in advance for shipment. Therefore they contain more of the nutrients necessary for the life forces.

For those of us who can get garden fresh vegetables, to preserve their true delicate flavor, as well as their natural sugars and nutrients, and to enjoy green vegetables at their wholesome best, they should be washed just before cooking, cooked just after picking (just to the point of doneness, not a moment more), and eaten just off the heat.

If vegetables are cooked at all, they should be prepared with a minimal loss of valuable nutrients. Listed here in the order of most nutrient value:

1. Clean, washed (never soaked), eaten raw
2. Steamed for 8 to 12 minutes in patapar paper
3. Pressure cooked with ½ cup water
4. Baked in covered dish with least water possible for preparation
The Oriental method of cooking vegetables is easy and retains

value. Simply heat a small amount of oil in a heavy skillet until oil is hot but not smoking. Choose young, crisp vegetables; shred, dice, or chop. The vegetables are then added to the oil, stirred for two or three minutes, then removed and served immediately. They are still brightly colored and crunchy.

Jerusalem Artichokes

2 lb. Jerusalem artichokes	Dash of cayenne
1 tsp. mild vinegar	2 tbsp. chopped parsley
2 to 3 tbsp. butter	

Stem artichokes and cook covered, in boiling water and vinegar, until tender. Test with a toothpick after 15 minutes. Drain. Melt butter, add seasoning, pour over artichokes.

Bean Dinner

2 C. cooked corn	1 tsp. paprika
2 C. cooked soy beans	2 tsp. molasses
2 C. lightly drained canned tomatoes	1 tbsp. grated onion

Combine all ingredients and place in a greased baking dish. Sprinkle the top with grated peanuts; bake covered, for about 45 minutes, at 350°.

Green Bean Casserole

3 pkg. frozen green beans	
2 C. grated Monterey Jack cheese	6 fresh tomatoes, sliced
2 C. cracked wheat or whole wheat bread crumbs	2 C. tomato juice

Butter pan and layer the ingredients alternately, ending with the cheese on top. Bake for 45 minutes at 350°.

Minted Green Beans

5 C. cooked fresh green beans
¼ C. chopped mint

⅓ C. butter, melted

Combine beans with other ingredients, heat, and serve.

Lima Bean Casserole

3 pkg. frozen lima beans
2 C. cracked wheat or whole
   wheat bread crumbs

6 fresh tomatoes, sliced
2 C. tomato juice
2 C. Monterey Jack cheese

Butter pan and layer ingredients alternately with cheese on top. Bake for 45 minutes at 350°.

Lima Beans with Cheese

3 tbsp. butter
¼ C. minced onion
1 lb. cheese, grated
4 C. cooked lima beans

1 tsp. dried basil
A few grains cayenne
1 C. chopped nut meats

Sauté onion in butter; stir in cheese over low heat until melted. Add beans, basil, cayenne, and nuts. Bake at 350° for about 30 minutes.

Bean Cake

Bean cake is known as soya cheese or Tofu. It is a precipitation of soy bean milk. You use bean cake about the same way as cottage cheese. It can be sprinkled on salads and soup.

2 C. soy flour (with the
   fat left in flour
2 C. cold water

4 C. boiling water
Juice of 4½ lemons

Beat soy flour into cold water with mixer. Pour the mixture in the boiling water, cooking for about 8 minutes. Add lemon juice. Cool and strain. Pack in a square container so it can be easily cut. Bean cake will keep for a week if you cut it and pour cold water over it and put in refrigerator, covered.

Bean Cake (Tofu) with Onions

1 onion, chopped	1 tsp. arrowroot
2 tbsp. peanut oil	1 tsp. soy sauce
½ lb. bean cake	¼ C. water

Sauté onions slightly in oil. Drain bean cake and cut in small cubes. Add bean cake to onions and stir. Mix arrowroot, soy sauce, and water. Pour over bean cake mixture. Simmer and stir until well heated and sauce is thickened.

Baked Beets

Fresh beets	Paprika to taste
Salt to taste	¼ C. melted butter

Preheat oven to 325°. Wash beets and trim the tops, leaving 2 inches of stem. Place on a pan and bake until tender. Pull off the skins. Season the beets with salt, paprika, and melted butter.

Pickled Beets

1 qt. sliced cooked beets	¼ C. cider vinegar
¼ C. pickling spices	

Drain beet juice into a small saucepan. Add pickling spices and cider vinegar. Heat this till it boils. Lower heat and simmer for about 4 to 5 minutes. Place beets in a small bowl. Strain liquid over beets and chill.

Brussels Sprouts

2 lb. brussels sprouts	1 C. tomato purée
3 C. water	Salt and pepper
2 tsp. brown sugar	2 tbsp. minced parsley

Cook brussels sprouts in boiling water. While they cook, combine other ingredients except parsley and bring to a boil. Drain sprouts, pour over the hot tomato sauce, and sprinkle with minced parsley.

Beet Greens

4 C. chopped beet greens	¼ tsp. salt
1 C. water	½ C. cultured sour cream
1 tsp. grated onion	

Simmer everything except sour cream 30 minutes. Remove from the heat and add sour cream.

Bulgur Pilaf

2 C. bulgur	½ lb. green peas
1 qt. boiling water	1 C. strong chicken stock
¼ lb. butter	1 lg. onion, chopped and sautéed
½ lb. mushrooms	in a little butter

Place bulgur in boiling water with butter and cover. Let set until double. Stir in remaining ingredients and cover. Bake at 325° for 1 hour.

Sautéed Cabbage

1 cabbage	1 tbsp. minced garlic or onion
2 tbsp. butter or oil	

Shred and chop cabbage. Heat butter or oil, sauté onion or garlic and shredded cabbage until tender, but still slightly crisp.

Baked Carrots

2 lb. baby carrots	¼ C. butter

Scrub carrots with vegetable brush, leaving them whole. Cook in a little water until tender. Arrange carrots in pan with butter and brown in 475° oven.

Carrot Loaf

6 C. mashed cooked carrots
1 C. organic peanut butter

½ stick butter, melted

Combine carrots and peanut butter in mixer. Pour into buttered loaf pan and bake for 45 minutes at 350°.

Celery Casserole

3 C. diagonally cut celery,
   including tops
2 C. chicken stock
½ C. slivered almonds

½ C. whole wheat bread crumbs
4 tbsp. butter, melted
¼ pimiento, chopped

Cook celery for a few minutes until almost tender in chicken stock. Combine all other ingredients with celery and pour into a greased casserole and bake at 350° for 30 minutes.

Celery Soufflé

3 tbsp. butter
5 tbsp. soy flour
2 C. non-fat milk
1 tsp. salt

Dash pepper
5 eggs, separated
1 C. finely diced celery,
   sautéed in 2 tbsp. butter

Melt butter, remove from heat, and blend in flour and a little of the milk until smooth. Add rest of milk and cook over direct heat, stirring constantly until sauce boils and thickens. Add seasonings. Beat egg yolks thoroughly, then gradually stir in the hot sauce and the celery. Beat egg whites until stiff and fold in cooled sauce lightly but thoroughly. Turn into a 6-cup ungreased casserole. Bake in a moderately slow oven, 325°.

Eggplant Casserole

3 tbsp. olive oil
2 eggs
1 onion, chopped fine
1 lb. fresh mushrooms, sliced
¼ tsp. sage

¼ tsp. poultry seasoning
2 eggplants, sliced
2 C. grated Monterey Jack cheese
¼ C. rye bread crumbs

Grease casserole dish with half of olive oil. Mix eggs, onions, mushrooms, and seasoning together. Alternate layers of eggplant, mixture, cheese, continuing in this manner, ending with cheese on top. Sprinkle with bread crumbs and bake at 350° for 40 minutes.

Eggplant "Kiss of Wine"

6 tomatoes, peeled
1 lg. onion, chopped
2 garlic cloves, finely chopped
2 bell peppers, finely chopped
1 tbsp. sweet basil
1 tbsp. oregano
½ C. red wine

¼ C. olive oil
2 tbsp. olive oil
4 lg. or 6 medium eggplants
2 C. grated Monterey Jack or
   Swiss cheese
¼ C. grated Parmesan cheese

Combine peeled tomatoes, onion, garlic, peppers, herbs, a kiss of wine (¼ C.), and oil in a large skillet. Simmer until the aroma asks for another kiss of wine. In another skillet, fry eggplant on both sides in 2 tbsp. oil; layer in casserole dish alternately with cheese and sauce, ending with sauce. Bake at 350° until bubbly.

Eggplant Slices

2 lg. unpeeled eggplants, sliced
¼ C. olive oil (optional)

2½ C. chopped spinach
¾ C. grated Gruyere cheese

Sauté eggplant in oil, or broil until tender. Place in oiled glass baking dish alternately with spinach and cheese, ending with cheese. Broil until cheese melts.

Enchiladas

1½ lb. Cheddar or Longhorn
cheese, grated
1½ lb. onions, diced
¼ C. vegetable oil

3 C. enchilada sauce plus 1 C.
water
1 C. sliced black olives
(save juice from cans)
2 doz. flour or corn tortillas

Combine grated cheese and onion in bowl. Heat vegetable oil in one frying pan, sauce and water in another. Fry tortillas in oil, then dip into sauce. Fill with cheese mixture, roll, and place in ungreased baking pan. Put any leftover ingredients except oil on top of enchiladas when all 24 have been put in pan; pour extra sauce on top, sprinkle with olives, and pour olive juice over enchiladas. Bake at 350° for 30 to 40 minutes until bubbly hot. From Gladys McGarey, Phoenix, Arizona.

Gnocchi

1 C. corn meal
3 C. boiling water
1 tsp. salt
½ tsp. cayenne
1 C. grated Sardo or
Parmesan cheese

2 tbsp. butter
½ tsp. dry mustard
2 eggs, beaten
4 tbsp. olive oil
½ C. whole wheat bread crumbs

Sprinkle the corn meal slowly into the rapidly boiling water with the salt and cayenne. Cook for 15 minutes, stirring continuously. Next remove from heat and stir in cheese, butter, mustard, and eggs. Pour into a rinsed shallow pan and chill well. Cut into squares, brush both sides with olive oil, and sprinkle cheese on top; broil until lightly browned.

Baked Kohlrabi

Quarter unpeeled kohlrabi. Season with butter and mace, wrap in aluminum foil, and bake at 350° until tender, about 20 minutes.

Lettuce and Rice

2 tbsp. butter	1 C. cooked brown rice
4 C. shredded lettuce outer leaves	2 C. tomato pulp or
½ C. finely chopped onion	thick stewed tomatoes
1 green pepper, chopped	Salt and pepper

Melt butter; cook lettuce, onion, and pepper gently in covered pan, about 10 minutes. Stir frequently, add other ingredients, and cook until well heated.

Millet Casserole

2 C. millet	2 lb. fresh tomatoes,
1 qt. boiling water	peeled and chopped
¼ lb. butter	2 C. grated Monterey Jack cheese
1 C. chopped celery	Vegetable salt to taste
1 C. chopped onion	

Place millet in boiling water with half of butter and let stand until double in bulk. Sauté onion, celery, and tomatoes in other half of butter. Combine all ingredients together and serve. If you prefer, bake covered for 20 minutes or so.

Mushroom Casserole

5 C. sliced fresh mushrooms	1 tbsp. oregano
1 lg. onion, diced	2 tbsp. brewers yeast
½ C. diced or sliced celery	½ C. water
½ C. finely chopped pimiento	Grated cheese
2 tbsp. corn oil	

Sauté vegetables in oil briefly. Add remaining ingredients except cheese. Pour in casserole dish and sprinkle with cheese. Cover and bake at 350° for about 25 minutes; uncover and cook 5 minutes more.

Nut Casserole

1 C. whole wheat bread crumbs	½ C. finely chopped green pepper
1 C. chopped celery	3 eggs, beaten
½ C. chopped parsley	2 C. non-fat milk
1 C. chopped English walnuts	Salt and pepper to taste
or pecans	3 tbsp. melted butter
1 lg. onion, chopped fine	

Combine crumbs, celery, parsley, nuts, onions, and green peppers. Add eggs and milk and mix together; season to taste. Pour in greased casserole dish and pour melted butter over. Bake at 325° for 1 hour.

Nut Loaf

Serve with broccoli or any green leafy vegetable.

3 tbsp. butter	1 egg, beaten
1 onion, minced	2 tbsp. chopped parsley
½ C. bread crumbs	¾ tsp. salt
1 C. chopped tomatoes	¼ tsp. paprika
1 C. chopped nuts,	1 tsp. grated lemon peel
preferably walnuts	

Preheat oven to 375°. Sauté onion in butter until soft. Combine with other ingredients in a greased baking dish. Bake for 20 minutes, then brown under the broiler. Serve with tomato sauce.

Creamed Onions

¼ C. butter	½ C. whole wheat flour
2 lg. onions, sliced lengthwise	1 C. canned milk
3 tbsp. butter	Dash or 2 of paprika

Sauté onions until tender. Melt 3 tbsp. butter; stir in flour until smooth. Add milk and heat thoroughly until sauce is thickened. Add onions and season to taste.

Stuffed Onions

6 lg. onions	¼ C. peanut butter
½ C. diced green pepper	¼ tsp. garlic juice
1 tbsp. butter	1½ tsp. salt
1 eight oz. can tomato sauce	3 C. cooked brown rice

Peel onions without cutting off root end. Cut a slice about 1 inch thick from the top of the onion. Place onions in large amount of boiling salted water and cook over moderate heat until tender. Drain and cool. Scoop out center of onions to form cups, leaving a half-inch shell. Save centers. Sauté green peppers in butter until crisp. Add ½ cup chopped reserved onion centers. Cook for a few minutes in remaining ingredients, except rice. Cook stirring until smooth. Add rice and mix. Fill onions with mixture. Bake in dish for 20 minutes at 350°.

Soybean Casserole

2 C. soybeans	1 small onion, chopped
Vegetable salt to taste	2 tbsp. molasses
A few peppercorns	2 tbsp. minced parsley
1 tsp. dry mustard	

Cover the beans with water and soak overnight. Drain, cover with fresh water, heat to the boiling point and simmer until tender, about 2 hours. They will double in bulk. Rub a casserole dish with butter. Mix the beans with all other ingredients. Set oven on 250° and let bake all day, at least eight hours.

Soybean Loaf I

1 C. grated carrots	1 C. tomato juice
2 C. soybeans (cooked or soaked overnight and whirled in blender until fine and mushy)	3 eggs
	4 tsp. soy flour
	1 tsp. sweet basil
1 onion, grated	1 tbsp. parsley
2 C. grated raw beets	Salt to taste
1 green pepper, minced	½ C. wheat germ

Mix all ingredients together well. Bake in an oiled loaf pan for 1½ hours at 325°.

Soybean Loaf II

2 C. soybeans (cooked or soaked
overnight and whirled in
blender until fine)
2 C. peeled and chopped
fresh tomatoes
2 tbsp. honey

¼ C. chopped onion
3 eggs
1 green pepper, chopped
3 tbsp. soy flour
¼ C. chopped ripe olives
1 C. tomato juice

Blend together all ingredients except tomato juice and cook in oiled loaf pan for 1 hour at 325°. Sprinkle top with tomato juice.

Soybean Patties

2 C. cooked soybeans,
ground and mashed
¼ C. chopped parsley
2 egg yolks, beaten
¼ tsp. pepper

1 tsp. salt
¼ C. whole wheat flour
2 tbsp. butter
2 tbsp. cream

Combine beans, onion, and parsley. Beat together egg yolks, cream, and seasonings; add to bean mixture and shape these into balls. Flatten them, dip in flour, and chill the patties for 1 hour or more. Saute them slowly in butter until brown. Serve them with any tomato sauce.

Spinach and Mushrooms

1½ lb. fresh mushrooms, sliced
2 lb. fresh spinach, chopped
3 tbsp. butter
½ onion, chopped

1 C. water
6 C. cooked brown rice
Yogurt or soy sauce

Sauté mushrooms, spinach, and onion in butter until tender. Add water, stirring for 5 minutes more. Serve over rice with yogurt or soy sauce.

Spinach Soufflé

3 pkg. frozen spinach	¼ lb. butter, melted
6 eggs, separated	1 C. chopped black walnuts

Thaw spinach and set aside. Whip egg whites until stiff. Combine butter, spinach, egg yolks, and black walnuts. Beat mixture with a wire whip. Fold in egg whites. Bake in a soufflé dish at 400° for about 20 minutes, until light and fluffy.

Spinach, Tomato, and Cheese Loaf

2 C. cooked spinach	Juice of ½ onion
2¼ C. canned tomatoes	¼ tsp. freshly ground pepper
½ lb. cheese, grated	2 hard-cooked eggs, chopped
1 C. cracker crumbs	

Toss ingredients until they are blended. Place in greased loaf pan. Bake at 350° for about 1 hour. Serve garnished with chopped eggs.

Sprout and Vegetable Salad

12 slices whole wheat bread	1 tbsp. lemon juice
1 stick butter, softened	1 tbsp. basil leaves
2 C. chopped cooked chick peas	6 lettuce leaves
½ C. chopped scallions	2 C. mung bean sprouts
3 tbsp. mayonnaise	12 tomato slices

Butter bread. In a bowl, combine chick peas, scallions, mayonnaise, juice, and basil. Place lettuce leaves on buttered sides of 6 slices of bread. Top with chick pea mixture, sprouts, 2 tomato slices each and the remaining slice of bread buttered side down. Cut in half.

Squash au Gratin

10 squash
2 onions, sliced
½ C. water

2 slices whole wheat bread crumbs
½ C. butter
1 C. grated Cheddar cheese

Wash squash, trim ends, and slice. Sauté with onions, butter, and water for 10 minutes until crisp. Add bread crumbs and spoon into serving bowl. Sprinkle grated cheese over squash.

Squash Casserole

3 pkg. frozen squash
2 C. cracked wheat or whole wheat bread crumbs

6 fresh tomatoes, sliced
2 C. tomato juice
3 C. grated Monterey Jack cheese

Layer ingredients alternately in a buttered pan, ending with cheese. Bake for 45 minutes at 350°.

Sautéed Squash

4 C. sliced squash
1 lg. onion, sliced

¼ C. butter
Paprika to taste

Wash squash; trim ends and slice without peeling. Add squash to onions and butter and sauté until tender; add paprika to taste.

Summer Squash

3 tbsp. corn oil or butter
1 onion, sliced
1 lg. tomato, chopped
4 unpeeled yellow squash, sliced

1 tsp. lemon juice
Salt to taste
Paprika

Sauté onions in oil or butter for 2 or 3 minutes. Add tomato and squash. Cover, cook over low heat for 15 to 20 minutes. Season and sprinkle a little paprika and serve.

Candied Sweet Potatoes

6 sweet potatoes baked in their jackets	1 C. dark corn syrup
1 tbsp. lemon juice	Powdered mace to taste

Remove jackets from potatoes and slice. Place potatoes in baking pan and pour over a lemon juice-corn syrup mixture. Bake for 15 minutes. Sprinkle a little mace over.

Stuffed Sweet Potatoes

6 lg. sweet potatoes	½ C. sweet heavy cream
3 tbsp. butter	

Scrub sweet potatoes well and bake at 350° until done. Gently open potatoes at one end and remove pulp and mash with other ingredients; refill and bake at 350° for 10 minutes more. Cut in half lengthwise and serve hot.

Swiss Chard Ring

3 tbsp. butter, melted	2 C. chopped cooked Swiss chard
3 tbsp. soy flour	1 C. grated Swiss cheese
1 C. non-fat milk	1 tbsp. onion juice
4 eggs	Vegetable salt to taste

Blend flour into butter over medium heat. Add milk. Cook until thickened, stirring constantly. Add eggs, Swiss chard, cheese, and onion juice. Sprinkle in soy flour and vegetable salt. Mix together and pour in oiled mold. Set mold into hot water and bake slowly for 40 minutes. Fill with vegetables or creamed chicken or fish.

Scalloped Tomatoes

4 C. stewed tomatoes	1 C. dry bread crumbs
Few drops onion juice	2 tbsp. butter

Season tomatoes with onion juice. Place ½ C. crumbs in bottom of baking dish; add tomatoes, cover with remaining crumbs and dot with butter. Bake at 475° for 20 minutes.

Stewed Tomatoes

2 lb. tomatoes	2 tsp. honey
1 C. water	1 tbsp. butter

Wash tomatoes, peel, and cut into pieces. Place in saucepan with water, cover tightly to prevent escape of steam, and cook slowly about 15 minutes, stirring occasionally. Season with salt, pepper, honey, and butter.

Baked Turnips

2 lb. turnips	1½ tsp. honey
¼ C. butter	½ C. water
1½ tsp. salt	

Pare turnips and cut into cubes. Place in baking dish with remaining ingredients. Cover closely and bake at 350° until tender.

Chinese Vegetables

2 onions, sliced	1 C. sliced mushrooms
4 green peppers, sliced	¼ C. oil or butter
4 celery stalks with tops, sliced	

Sauté vegetables quickly in hot oil or butter. Remove from pan and stir in a little soy sauce or ¼ recipe of Chinese gravy.

Egg Foo Young

8 eggs, beaten	2 celery stalks including
3 scallions, sliced	tops, minced
1½ C. bean sprouts	1 recipe of Chinese gravy

Add all the vegetables to beaten eggs and stir together. Cook the mixture in a lightly oiled pre-heated frying pan as you would pancakes, turning once. Place in a shallow casserole dish and cover with Chinese gravy. Serve over cooked rice with a little soy sauce if desired.

Chinese Gravy

3 C. water
¼ C. soy sauce

2½ tbsp. arrowroot

Blend ingredients together and cook over double boiler until thickened, stirring every few minutes.

Baked Root Vegetables

8 small carrots
8 small potatoes
8 small onions
¾ tsp. salt

⅛ tsp. pepper
1 C. melted cheese
2 tbsp. butter

Pare carrots and potatoes and cut into slices. Peel onions and mince. Combine vegetables in greased baking dish, season with salt and pepper, add cheese, and dot with butter. Bake at 350° for 15 minutes.

Vegetable Chow Mein

1 stick butter
1 stalk celery
1 lg. onion
3 bell peppers
1 Chinese cabbage

2 whole pimientos, chopped
1 C. fresh mushrooms
2 C. cold water
¼ C. arrowroot
¼ C. soy sauce

Slice all vegetables in julienne strips. Sauté in butter in this order: celery, onion, bell peppers, Chinese cabbage, mushrooms; adding all together with 2 C. water and arrowroot. Pour in soy sauce and add pimientos.

Vegetable Loaf

½ C. cooked peas
½ C. cooked string beans
½ C. chopped cooked carrots
1½ C. milk
1 egg

1 C. soft whole wheat
   bread crumbs
½ tsp. salt
⅛ tsp. pepper
½ tsp. paprika

Press peas through a sieve, cut beans into small pieces, and combine all vegetables. Add milk, slightly beaten egg, crumbs, and seasoning. Turn into greased baking dish and bake at 350° until firm.

Vegetable Pie

3 medium onions, chopped
3 medium green peppers,
   chopped
⅓ C. butter
6 medium tomatoes, diced

1½ C. corn
⅛ tsp. pepper
1 baked pastry shell
¼ C. grated cheese
1 tsp. salt

Cook onions and peppers in butter five minutes. Add tomatoes and corn and cook 10 minutes longer, but do not brown. Season. Fill pastry shell and sprinkle with cheese.

Zucchini Casserole

1 tbsp. oregano
1 tbsp. thyme
1 tbsp. sweet basil
3 C. canned tomatoes

¼ C. olive oil
6 unpeeled zucchini, sliced
2 C. whole wheat bread cubes
2 C. grated Swiss cheese

Mix seasoning with tomato and olive oil in blender and blend for a few seconds. Put half of zucchini and 1 C. bread cubes in casserole dish and pour half of tomato mixture over. Sprinkle 1 C. of Swiss cheese. Add the rest of zucchini and bread cubes. Pour the second half of tomato mixture over. Sprinkle the remaining Swiss cheese on top and bake at 325° for 1 hour.

Stuffed Zucchini

3 zucchini
2 tbsp. minced onion
3 tbsp. butter
1 C. melted cheese

1 C. soft whole wheat
bread crumbs
½ C. cooked tomatoes

Cook whole zucchini in boiling water for 5 minutes. Cut in halves and scoop out centers. Mix pulp with remaining ingredients. Fill zucchini and bake in oven 350° for 10 minutes.

Zucchini and Tomatoes Au Gratin

2 lb. zucchini
3 tbsp. chopped onions
3 tbsp. olive oil

2 C. chopped fresh tomatoes
⅛ tsp. pepper
¾ C. grated cheese

Wash zucchini and cut into ¼-inch pieces. Sauté onions in olive oil and add zucchini, cooking slowly for 5 minutes; stir frequently. Add tomatoes and pepper; cover and cook for 5 minutes longer. Turn into greased baking dish. Sprinkle cheese over top and bake in moderate oven, 375°, about 5 minutes.

Zucchini in Tomato Sauce

5 tomatoes, quartered
¼ C. butter
½ tsp. salt

⅛ tsp. pepper
1 lb. fresh zucchini
2 tbsp. chopped parsley

Peel tomatoes and stew in butter until cooked to a thick sauce, stirring constantly. Season with salt and pepper. Wash zucchini, dice very fine, add to tomato sauce, and simmer about 15 minutes or until tender. Sprinkle with parsley.

Salmagundi Bake

½ C. dry soy beans	1½ tsp. seasoned salt
2 C. water	¼ tsp. tabasco sauce
1 C. boiling water	1 lg. Monterey Jack or
1 C. uncooked bulgur or	Swiss cheese, sliced
cracked wheat	1 one lb. 14 oz. can whole
½ C. chopped onions	tomatoes, chopped
½ C. chopped green peppers	1 tsp. ground cumin

Soak soy beans overnight in 2 C. water. After soaked, drain beans, return 1 C. water and blend in blender until smooth (or grind beans in grinder, then afterwards add 1 C. water). Pour 1 C. boiling water over bulgur, onion, peppers, seasoned salt, and tabasco sauce. Mix tomatoes and cumin. Butter 3 qt. casserole. Layer half of bulgur mix, half of cheese, half of tomato and cumin mixture; repeat. Bake covered at 375° for 15 minutes. Serves 6. From Grethe Tedrick of Point Richmond, California, an A.R.E. member. One delightful way to add soy beans to your diet.

RICE DISHES

Rice is at its best when baked, particularly brown and wild rice. The ratio of water is 4 C. water to 1 C. rice with a little butter or olive oil sprinkled on top. Cover tightly and bake at 375° until tender, approximately 45 minute to 1 hour. This method is easy and keeps nutrients in.

Baked Green Rice

1 egg	1 sm. onion, minced
½ C. milk	2 C. cooked brown rice
½ C. finely chopped parsley	½ C. grated sharp cheese
1 clove garlic, finely chopped	½ tsp. curry powder

Mix ingredients well in a baking dish in which has been poured 2 tbsp. olive oil. Bake for 30 to 40 minutes.

Wild Rice Ring

1 C. cooked wild rice
1 clove garlic, sliced
¼ C. butter

½ tsp. poultry seasoning or
   freshly grated nutmeg
1 C. sautéed onions
   and mushrooms

Combine ingredients and place in a well-greased 7-inch ring mold in a pan of hot water and bake for about 20 minutes. Loosen the edges with a knife, invert the contents onto a platter, and fill the center with: sautéed onions and mushrooms.

Cheese Rice

1 C. brown sugar
3 C. water
½ to ¾ C. or more grated cheese

¼ tsp. paprika
A few grains cayenne

Bake rice in water; whn water is nearly absorbed, add other ingredients, stirring to combine. Finish cooking rice.

Wild Rice and Mushrooms

⅓ C. sliced mushrooms
1 C. beef broth
1 medium onion, finely chopped
1 C. wild rice

1 C. brown rice
2 tbsp. butter
2 tbsp. snipped parsley

Combine mushrooms and beef broth, add water to make 2 C. In saucepan bring broth mixture and onions to boiling. Add washed wild rice; reduce heat, simmer 20 minutes. Add brown rice; return to boiling, then reduce heat, cover, and simmer 20 minutes longer or till rice is done. Add mushrooms and butter, heat briefly, add parsley.

Rice with Spinach and Chestnuts

2 C cooked brown rice
2 C. cooked chopped spinach
1 C. cooked chestnuts

1 C. grated cheese
Watercress
Pimiento

Combine rice, spinach, chestnuts, and cheese, and bake about 30 minutes or until thoroughly heated. Garnish with sprigs of watercress and ribbons of pimiento before serving.

Shish Kabob, Brown Rice

2 lb. lamb
½ C. red wine
¼ C. oil
1 onion, diced
1 clove garlic, minced
Salt, pepper, oregano to taste

3 green peppers, cut in chunks
3 tomatoes, cut in quarters
Mushroom caps
2 tbsp. butter
¼ C. chopped onions
3 C. brown rice, cooked

Cut lamb into 1½ inch cubes. Combine wine, oil, onion, garlic, and seasonings; pour over lamb. Marinate at room temperature 2 hours or overnight in the refrigerator. Fill each skewer alternately with meat, pepper chunks, tomato wedges, and mushrooms. Brush with marinade. Broil quickly, close to heat, until done to taste. Serve on bed of brown rice.

Lamb Curry with Wild Rice

2 C. cooked, hot wild rice
1 C. sliced onion
¼ C. diced green pepper
1 c. diced celery
1 clove garlic, minced
4 tbsp. oil

3 C. diced cooked lamb
1 tsp. curry powder
1½ tsp. salt
2 C. lamb gravy
Chutney to taste

Keep rice hot. Sauté onion, green pepper, celery, and garlic in oil. Add remaining ingredients. Cover; cook about 30 minutes over low heat. Serve in border of cooked rice with chutney.

Brunswick Stew

2 qt. chicken stock
1 C. sliced celery
1 C. sliced carrots
12 to 15 whole baby onions
2 C. shelled green peas
1 lb. okra

3 C. fresh peeled, diced tomatoes
2 tbsp. sugar
2 C. fresh cut corn
2 C. brown rice

Combine all ingredients, except corn and rice, and simmer about 20 minutes, or until vegetables are tender. Add corn and rice. Simmer until rice is tender.

Vegetable Jambalaya

⅔ C. rice, cooked
1 lb. mushrooms, sautéed lightly in butter
2 medium-sized green peppers, chopped
1 medium onion, chopped
1 stalk celery, chopped

2 canned pimientos, chopped
1¼ C. cooked tomatoes, chopped
¾ tsp. salt
A few grains cayenne
½ tsp. paprika
¼ lb. butter, melted

Combine the rice and other ingredients. Place in a greased baking dish. Bake covered for about 1 hour.

EGGS

Eggs are nutritious, economical, usually quickly assembled, and can be served in any number of appealing combinations which are pleasing to the eye and to the palate.

We use organic eggs from Dr. Brewer's farm when possible, otherwise we get them from local farmers. Eggs that are fertile are the very best. Also, let me repeat, the yolks are alkaline forming and the whites are acid forming.

From Cayce reading 5399: Some elements in eggs are not found in other foods—particularly sulphur. Egg whites cause other elements in the diet to be bad; yet we would take them occasionally. Do not necessarily eat meat if you are that minded. But remember, it is not what goes in the mouth but what comes out of the mouth that defiles the body.

Omelet

4 eggs	¼ C. water
½ tsp. salt	2 tbsp. butter
Few grains pepper	

Beat eggs until mixed but not foamy; stir in seasonings and water. Melt butter in a heavy skillet and turn mixture into the hot skillet/ Cook omelet slowly, pricking and lifting with a fork during cooking period. Cook until firm to the touch of a finger, 8 minutes. The omelet may be cooked entirely on top of range or put in oven part of the time to dry the top. Fold omelet, then slide onto a hot platter. Serve immediately. Variations: Serve omelet with hot spinach, bacon, tomato sauce or hot broiled fruit such as peaches or apricots. A cooked vegetable or meat filling may be added before the omelet is folded.

Smoked Salmon with Eggs

Pumpernickel bread	Poached eggs
Butter	Dill seed
Smoked salmon (lox)	

Toast and butter 1 slice of bread per portion. Using one very thin slice of salmon per serving, dip each into boiling water, dry, and place on toast. Place a poached egg on each; sprinkle with dill.

Shirred Eggs

2 eggs
1 tsp. cream or melted butter

1 tsp. grated cheese (optional)

Preheat oven to 350°. For one serving grease a small baking dish or ramekin and carefully break in eggs. Add cream or melted butter. Bake for about 8 minutes. Garnish with cheese.

Baked Eggs on Toast

8 tsp. chopped celery
8 tsp. chopped chives
8 eggs
Salt

Paprika
4 rounds hot, buttered whole wheat toast

Preheat oven to 325°. Grease 4 warmed individual molds with butter and place 2 tsp. chopped celery, chives, and 2 eggs into each dish. Season them with salt and paprika to taste. Cover each mold with a small poaching paper. Place the molds in a pan of hot water, deep enough to reach to within ½ inch of the top. Bake until the eggs are firm. Turn them out on hot toast.

POULTRY

To clean: pick poultry dry or dip into hot, but not boiling, water until water penetrates to skin. Grasp feathers close to skin and pull in direction they grow, not against it. Cut off wing tips, if desired. Singe by holding dry bird over direct flame, turning to expose all parts of the body. Remove pinfeathers with tweezers, or use dull edge of knife.

Cut around vent and make slit almost to tip of breastbone. Insert hand and carefully loosen entrails from back and sides; pull out, making sure lungs are removed.

Push back skin of neck; cut off neck close to body; remove windpipe. Separate gizzard, heart, and liver; cut away gall bladder attached to liver, being careful not to break it. Cut through thickest part of gizzard; open and pull out sac. remove oil sac from tail. Rinse in cool water and dry with paper town, or drain.

Golden Broiled Chicken

2 broiling chickens	2 tbsp. melted butter or salad oil

Split broilers in half lengthwise. Brush with melted butter or salad oil. Place skin side up in broiler pan and broil 5-7 inches from heat for about 10 minutes. Turn and broil another 10 minutes. Turn again and broil about 10 minutes longer, basting with drippings. When drumstick moves easily and thickest part of chicken feels very soft, chicken is done.

Roast Stuffed Turkey

Stuff and truss turkey just before roasting. Allow about ¾ C. stuffing per pound of ready-to-cook weight. Spoon in stuffing. Shake bird to settle stuffing; do not pack.

Truss by placing skewers across opening and lace shut with cord. Tie drumsticks securely to tail. (If opening has band of skin across, push drumsticks underneath; you won't need to fasten opening or tie legs.)

Grease skin thoroughly with butter. If you use a meat thermometer, insert it in the center of the inside thigh muscle adjoining the cavity. Place breast up on a rack (put breast down if using a V-rack) in shallow roasting pan and leave in this position for entire roasting time. Cover with loose "cap" of aluminum foil, pressing it lightly at drumstick and breast ends, but avoid having it touch top or sides. Roast at constant low temperature, till done.

Roast Goose

Clean goose. Stuff with bread stuffing. Place breast up on rack in shallow roasting pan. Pour 2 C. boiling water over and cover. Roast at 325°about 25 to 30 minutes per pound. Prick legs and wings with fork so fat will run out. Roast uncovered last 15 minutes. To remove excess fat, goose may be precooked before roasting; boil for half an hour; save stock for gravy and fat for skin cream.

Stewed Chicken

Cut into pieces a 4 to 5 pound ready-to-cook chicken. Place back, wings, and legs on bottom of Dutch oven; top with the rest. Add water just to cover. (If chicken is for salad, add ½ C. water per pound.) Add a stalk of celery, a carrot, an onion, 4 peppercorns, 2 whole cloves, 2 whole allspice, 1 bay leaf, and ½ tsp. salt per pound of chicken.

Bring to boiling; reduce heat, cover, and simmer 3 to 4 hours or until tender. Remove chicken from broth; cool, refrigerate. Skim fat from broth.

Roast Duck

5-pound, ready-to-cook duck	2 tbsp. honey
Orange stuffing	1 tsp. Kitchen Bouquet

Remove wings, tips and first joints, leaving only meaty second joints. Rub inside with salt. Stuff lightly with stuffing (or with celery leaves and 1 tart apple, quartered). Don't prick skin or truss. Skewer opening; lace.

Place breast up on rack in shallow pan. Don't add water. Roast uncovered at 325°, 1½ to 2 hours for medium done. Leg will move easily. About 30 minutes before end of roasting time, brush with mixture of honey and Kitchen Bouquet.

Orange Stuffing

3 C. toasted bread cubes
2 C. finely diced celery
1 tbsp. grated orange peel
⅔ C. diced orange sections
¾ tsp. salt

½ tsp. poultry seasoning
Dash pepper
1 beaten egg
¼ C. melted butter

Toss together bread, celery, orange peel, orange sections, and seasonings. Combine egg and butter; add to bread mixture, tossing lightly. Makes enough stuffing for a 5 pound duck.

Bread Stuffing

5 C. toasted bread cubes
3 tbsp. chopped onions
1 tsp. salt
1 tsp. pepper

1 tbsp. poultry seasoning
Little sage to taste
¼ C. butter
Hot broth or water to moisten

Combine bread, onions, and seasoning. Add butter and enough liquid to moisten. Toss gently to mix.

Giblet Stuffing: To bread stuffing add chopped cooked giblets; use giblet broth as liquid.
Raisin Stuffing: To bread stuffing add ½ C. seedless raisins to bread mixture.
Celery Stuffing: Add 1 C. finely chopped celery. Cook in butter, if desired.
Chestnut Stuffing: Add 1 C. chopped celery and 2 C. boiled chestnuts, chopped; use milk for liquid.
Mushroom Stuffing: Add 1 C. sliced fresh mushrooms cooked in part of the butter.

Herb Stuffing

3 qt. slightly dry bread cubes
1½ tsp. ground sage
1½ tsp. thyme
1½ tsp. rosemary
1½ tsp. salt

⅓ C. chopped parsley
⅓ C. chopped onion
⅓ C. butter, melted
1 C. chicken broth

Combine bread, seasonings, parsley, onion, and butter. Add broth and toss lightly to mix. Makes 8 C. or enough stuffing for a 10 pound turkey.

Buckwheat Groat Stuffing

1 C. cooked buckwheat groats	½ C. sliced fresh mushrooms
2 ½ C. water	2 tbsp. chopped parsley
1 tsp. salt	1 small diced red bell pepper
3 tbsp. butter	or pimiento
½ C. diced celery and leaves	

Sauté celery, fresh mushrooms, parsley, and pepper or pimiento for 5 minutes in butter. Add to cooked buckwheat groats. Use for stuffing chicken, duck, or wild game fowl. Also good served in place of noodles or potatoes.

Baked Chicken Breast

8 to 10 boned chicken breasts	2 C. celery soup
1 clove garlic	1 lb. fresh mushrooms, sliced

Place chicken breasts in pan, cut side down. Squeeze juice from garlic into soup and pour over chicken. Add sliced mushrooms and bake at 350°for 45 minutes. Serve over rice or whole wheat toast.

FISH

Fresh fish has firm flesh that springs back when pressed with the finger tips. The eyes should be bright and full, the gills should be reddish pink. When possible, buy your fish alive or catch your own. Frozen fish should always be hard frozen. Smoked fish should be firm with a sweet, smokey odor.

When cleaning and scaling fish, first remove the fins by cutting into the flesh on both sides at the base of the fin. (Kitchen shears will do a fine job.) Scale the fish very well with a fork or fish scaler, holding the fish by the tail and working toward the head. Rinse in cold water. Cut the head off behind the gills. Slit the belly from end to end and remove all the entrails, being careful not to break the gall as this will leave a bad taste on the fish. Wash fish under cold running water and place in ice water until you are ready to prepare it. I add a little lemon juice to the water. Cook the same day.

When filleting fish, place the knife between the flesh and the end of the first rib bone at the head of a cleaned and scaled fish. Cut the flesh down the back bone, trying to leave as little meat behind as possible. Follow this process down both sides of the fish. Lift out the bone and head and use to make fish stock which can be frozen until ready for use.

Fresh Fish Baked in Parchment Paper

Fresh fish steaks or fillets or whole fish	Kelp
Melted butter	Paprika
Lemon juice	Parsley
	Soy Sauce

Use either whole fresh fish, fish steaks, or large fillets. Wash in cold water, rub melted butter all over, and sprinkle with a mixture of lemon juice, soy sauce, kelp, paprika, and parsley.

Place fish in center of parchment paper and fold paper neatly over the fish, leaving a hem around the edges that can be secured with a paper clip or pin. Bake at 350°, for 25 minutes. Slide cooked fish out on a hot platter, cut paper away with scissors, and let juices flow over fish. Garnish with lemon slices and crisp watercress or endive.

Cod Fish Au Gratin

Cod fillets	Seafood seasoning
Melted butter	Grated Parmesan cheese

Use fresh fillets of cod; rinse in cold water, brush with melted butter and sprinkle with a little seafood seasoning and Parmesan cheese. Broil for 15 minutes.

Salmon Steaks Au Gratin

6 Salmon steaks	1 C. grated Swiss cheese
½ C. non-fat milk	1 tsp. seafood seasoning

Cook milk, Swiss cheese, and seasoning in top of double boiler for 25 minutes. Pour sauce over salmon steaks and cook covered for 30 minutes in a 325° oven. Garnish and serve.

Salmon Cakes

2 C. canned salmon	⅛ tsp. paprika
½ C. whole wheat bread crumbs	½ C. peanut or corn oil
	2 beaten eggs

Combine these ingredients and form into cakes. Sauté them until brown, using a little oil as needed to prevent sticking.

Baked Big Blue

3 lb. fresh blue fish	1 lemon, sliced
3 tbsp. safflower oil	¼ C. soy sauce

Clean fish, wash in cold water and towel blot dry. Mix oil and soy sauce together. Place fish in oiled baking dish, brush with soy sauce mixture, and drop lemon slices over. Bake 350° for 25 minutes.

Herb-Baked Cod

2 lb. cod fillet	¼ tsp. thyme
1 tbsp. butter	Dash pepper
1 tsp. salt	1 small bay leaf
1 clove garlic, minced	½ C. thinly sliced onions,
¼ tsp. oregano	separated in rings

Place fish in baking dish, dot with butter and sprinkle with the seasonings. Add bay leaf, arrange onion rings over top of fish. Bake uncovered at 350° for about 30 minutes or until tender.

Creole Fillets

1 C. chopped onion	1½ tsp. salt
1 C. chopped green pepper	Dash of cayenne
4 C. canned tomatoes	2 lb. halibut fillets
3 tbsp. oil	1 tsp. pepper
1 or 2 bay leaves	

Sauté onion, green pepper, and garlic in hot oil until tender. Add tomatoes, bay leaf, salt, and dash cayenne; simmer 15 minutes. Place fish in baking dish. Sprinkle with 1 tsp. pepper. Pour tomato mixture over fish. Bake at 350° about 45 minutes or until tender.

MEATS

Meats should usually be roasted, baked, or broiled—never fried. Stewing is acceptable provided the broth is used, in which case a closely covered pan or dish should be used, and the food should be simmered rather than boiled.

Cook at low tempertaures for maximum nutritive value, digestibility, and flavor. High temperatures cause the meat fibers to contract, thus toughening and squeezing out the juices.

Edgar Cayce recommends wild game and organ meats as preferable to other meats. Fish, fowl, and lamb are easily digested meats.

The more tender cuts of all meats are the sections where the least body movements and stress occur. The cuts respond very well to roasting, broiling, baking, pan broiling, and sautéing.

Lamb Casserole

Stretching meats is not a new art. Chefs have been practicing this for many years and producing lovely foods.

4 lb. lean lamb	1 tsp. grated ginger
6 tbsp. butter	1 tsp. cardamon
2 lg. onions	1 C. raisins
2 cloves garlic, minced	1 tbsp. sea kelp
4 tbsp. whole wheat flour	1 tbsp. salt
3 C. water	6 yellow squash, cubed
1 tsp. cinnamon	½ C. fresh lemon juice

Cut meat into small strips and sauté in butter. Pour this in a large baking dish. Sauté onions and garlic. Stir in flour, water, cinnamon, ginger, cardamon, raisins, sea kelp and salt. Cook a few minutes while stirring constantly. Pour sauce over meat in the baking dish. Bake for 30 minutes. Add squash and lemon juice. Cook for 10 minutes more.

Leg of Lamb

This is a Marshalls favorite, so good you'll eat it to the bone.

1 tsp. chopped parsley	1 tsp. basil
1 tsp. minced garlic	1 tsp. salt
1 tsp. thyme	1 tsp. pepper
1 tsp. kelp	1 spring lamb leg
2 tsp. mint leaves	

Mix herbs and seasonings in a small bowl. Rub all over lamb leg. Bake at 325° until lamb shank begins to leave bone. Serve with mint jelly.

Breast of Lamb

6 lb. lamb breast	¼ C. prepared mustard
1 C. canned tomato sauce	¼ C. cider vinegar
¼ C. molasses	

Cut lamb, if needed, into serving-size pieces. Place in a single layer on a rack of the broiler pan. Bake at 350° for 1 hour. Pour off fat. Mix tomato sauce, molasses, mustard, and cider vinegar in a small bowl. Brush part of the mixture over ribs and coat well. continue baking and brushing ribs with more sauce. Turn in 1 hour and again 30 minutes later. Serve remaining sauce with ribs.

Lamb Chops

Lamb chops	Mint leaves
Melted butter	

Brush melted butter and sprinkle mint leaves on one side of lamb chops. Cook for 12 minutes at 375°. Repeat for other side. They will be tender and very juicy.

Roast Lamb with Dressing

1 lamb shoulder	2 C. celery, chopped
Salt, pepper, and curry powder to taste	8 C. whole wheat bread cubes
	3 tbsp. butter
Pinch or two of dry mustard	½ C. whole wheat flour
½ onion, chopped	2 tbsp. Kitchen Bouquet

Have butcher remove bone or remove it yourself. Cook the 2 qt. water with bone to make stock. Rub lamb inside and out with seasoning. Combine all the other ingredients for dressing, pour ½ C. of stock over and cook for 1 hour at 325°. Place dresssing inside of lamb and roll up and tie with small rope and bake for 2 hours at 325°, basting with lamb stock and 2 tbsp. of Kitchen Bouquet and ½ C. whole wheat flour whisked in with wire whip.

Roast Venison

3 to 4 lb. venison	¼ lb. butter, melted
1 C. red wine	

Place roast in a closed baking pan or use aluminum foil to seal with. Pour 1 C. of wine over meat and pour butter over wine. Roast at 325°, for 1 hour. Baste with drippings at 15 to 20 minute intervals.

Rabbit or Squirrel

Cut dressed rabbit in serving pieces. Disjoint legs at body and second joints. Check to see if tendons of left leg have been removed; if not, remove them. Split down center back and through breast, cutting each half in two. (Many folks like to soak meat in salted water for a few hours before cooking; drain.) Brush with melted butter. Bake slowly at 325° for 1 to 1½ hours. Sprinkle with water every 15 minutes until tender.

Sautéed Chicken Livers

2 lb. chicken livers
2 tbsp. corn oil
Dash or two salt and pepper

1 tbsp. celery seeds
½ C. whole wheat flour

Shake livers with dry ingredients in paper bag or container with lid. Sauté in corn oil 3 or 4 minutes on each side. Serve.

Baked Brains

2 pair lamb or beef brains
1 C. water
Juice of 1 lemon

Grated cheese
Salt and pepper to taste

Simmer brains in water for 25 minutes. Drain and chop. Sprinkle with lemon juice, grated cheese (I use a mixture of Swiss and Parmesan), salt and pepper to taste.

Broiled Lamb Kidney

8 lamb kidneys
½ C. melted butter

4 scallions, chopped
1 C. sliced fresh mushrooms

Before cooking, slice open and remove membrane and hard white parts from kidneys. Rinse. Place kidneys in shallow pan, brush with butter and broil for 10 minutes on each side. Sauté scallions and mushrooms in a saucepan in remaining butter, and pour over broiled kidneys.

Desserts

Desserts can balance a meal nutritionally. Also most families keep sweets on hand for snacks and treats. The desserts I have given here contain the best possible ingredients, and help supply the daily needs of vitamins, minerals, and protein. Some recipes are rich with natural fruit sweets, both fresh and dried.

When the meal is hearty, serve a light dessert such as a natural sweet. On the other hand, if the meal is predominatly vegetable, follow it with a dessert of eggs, cheese, milk, or yogurt.

A special word on raw sugar, since raw sugar was one of the sweets recommended by the Cayce Readings: raw sugar, maple syrup, and honey are acid-producing, they should be limited because an excess can produce an unhealthy imbalance. I can't stress enough the importance of balancing the meal.

Carob Fruit Cake

⅓ C. butter
1 C. raw sugar
½ C. Carob flour
⅓ C. blackstrap molasses
3 eggs, separated
½ C. water
1¼ C. whole wheat flour

3 tsp. Royal baking powder
¼ tsp. salt
1 tsp. cinnamon
½ C. chopped dates and raisins
⅓ C. chopped pecans
⅓ C. chopped English walnuts
1 tsp. vanilla extract

Preheat oven to 325°. Rub a loaf pan with oil and line it with waxed paper. Rub the paper with oil and sprinkle lightly with flour. Beat butter until soft. Combine sugar and carob flour and molasses, gradually adding to the butter. Beat until light and creamy. Add the egg yolks one at a time and beat well after each addition. Stir in water. Add 1 cup of flour with the baking powder, salt, and cinnamon, and beat into mixture. Sprinkle the remaining flour over the fruits and nuts and stir into batter. Add vanilla and mix well. Add stiffly beaten egg shites. Pour mixture into loaf pan and bake for about 1 hour. Let cool in pan.

Ginger Bread

2 C. whole wheat flour
2 tsp. Royal baking powder
½ tsp. baking soda
½ tsp. salt
1 tsp. grated ginger
1 tsp. cinnamon

1 tsp. ground cloves
1 C. sour cream
2 eggs, beaten
1 C. honey
½ C. melted butter
¾ C. water

Stir dry ingredients together. Mix sour cream, eggs, and honey together with melted butter and water. Combine all of the ingredients together and beat thoroughly. Pour into a greased and floured loaf pan and bake at 350°, for 35 minutes, or until crusty on top.

Honey Cake

2 C. unsifted whole wheat
   pastry flour
2 tsp. Royal baking powder
½ tsp. salt
½ C. butter or corn oil

1 C. honey
2 eggs
½ C. non-fat milk
1 tsp. vanilla

Stir dry ingredients together. Cream butter or oil and honey together; add eggs and beat well. Add dry ingredients slowly, alternately with milk, stirring only enough to blend. Add vanilla. Bake in greased and floured loaf or square pan 350°, for 35 minutes.

Baked Brown Rice Custard

2 thirteen oz. cans evaporated
 milk
1 lb. brown sugar or
1½ C. honey
1 lb. brown rice, cooked

2 tbsp. cinnamon
1 tbsp. nutmeg
2 tbsp. vanilla
6 eggs
½ C. hot cream

Mix milk with equal parts of water, sugar or honey, and rice. Mix dry
ingredients and vanilla and combine with milk mixture. Beat eggs and add a
small amount of hot cream to beaten eggs, stirring constantly. Combine all
ingredients and mix thoroughly. Pour into buttered pan and bake at 375°, for
one hour.

Sour Cream Ginger Bread

2 C. boiling water
1 C. seedless raisins
1 C. sour cream
½ C. melted butter
½ C. brown sugar
½ C. honey
½ C. blackstrap molasses

2 eggs
3½ C. whole wheat flour
2 tsp. baking soda
2 tsp. grated ginger
2 tsp. cinnamon
1 tsp. ground allspice

Preheat oven to 375°. Pour boiling water over the raisins and let stand 5
minutes. Drain and cool. Combine sour cream, butter, sugar, honey,
molasses, and eggs, and beat well. Add the raisins and mix. Add dry
ingredients, mixing thoroughly. Pour into greased and floured pan. Bake 30
minutes until top is crusty.

Fruit Cake

1 C. butter
½ C. honey
½ C. brown sugar
½ C. blackstrap molasses
2 eggs
2 C. whole wheat flour
2 tsp. Royal baking powder
½ tsp. mace
½ tsp. nutmeg
½ tsp. allspice
½ tsp. cinnamon
½ C. dates, pitted & chopped
½ C. chopped pecans
½ C. seedless raisins
¼ C. each grated orange and
lemon peel

Beat butter until soft; cream with honey, brown sugar, and molasses. Add eggs one at a time and beat thoroughly after each addition. Stir 2 C. whole wheat flour with baking powder, mace, nutmeg, allspice, and cinnamon. Combine fruits and nuts; coat with ¼ C. of the flour mixture. Mix the remaining flour mixture with the creamed ingredients. Alternate batter and fruit mix in thirds in a greased and floured Bundt pan or 2 medium loaf pans. Bake 1¼ hours at 325°. If cake browns too quickly, cover pan with brown paper. Cool in pan.

Tube Spice Cake

¾ C. butter
2 C. raw sugar
3 eggs
3 C. buckwheat flour
2 tsp. Royal baking powder
½ tsp. baking soda
1 tsp. cinnamon
1 tsp. nutmeg
1 tsp. ginger
1 tsp. ground cloves
½ C. grated Brazil nuts
¾ C. buttermilk

Preheat oven to 350°. Oil a tube pan and sprinkle in a little flour. Turn pan upside down and shake out excess flour. Beat butter and sugar until light and fluffy. Add eggs and beat about 1 minute. Combine all dry ingredients. Add alternately with the buttermilk to the wet ingredients. Beat until light and fluffy. Pour into pan and bake about 1 hour, until center springs back, or toothpick comes out clean.

Carob Cake

½ C. soft margarine or butter	2½ C. whole wheat flour
2 C. brown sugar	½ tsp. soda
2 eggs	½ tsp. cream of tartar
½ C. carob powder	½ C. yogurt
½ C. water	⅓ C. non-fat milk

Cream together the sugar and the margarine; beat eggs in well. Add the water and the carob powder. Beat. Stir together flour, soda, and cream of tartar. Gradually add the dry mixture and beat after each addition. Alternately add the yogurt and the milk. Beat the cake mixture for 1 minute more. Pour the batter in a greased and floured pan of your choice. Bake at 350° for 30 to 35 minutes until done. Serve with your favorite sauce.

Fig Cake

½ C. corn oil	3 tsp. Royal baking powder
2 C. brown sugar	¼ tsp. salt
4 eggs	1 tsp. cinnamon
3 C. chopped figs	1 tsp. ginger
3 C. whole wheat flour	1 C. water

Blend the corn oil with the brown sugar. Add the eggs and the chopped figs. Mix well. Stir the dry ingredients together. Add alternately, with the water, to the fig mixture. Beat well after each addition. Pour into a greased and floured tube pan. Bake at 325°, for 1½ hours.

Baked Peach Tapioca

½ C. tapioca	1 C. water
½ C. honey	1 tbsp. lemon juice
1 tsp. nutmeg	2 tbsp. melted butter
3 C. cubed fresh peaches	

Mix tapioca, honey, and nutmeg. Heat the peaches and the water with the lemon juice in a sauce pan. Stir in the tapioca mixture. Heat to boiling point, remove from heat, add the butter. Bake at 350°, in a buttered square pan for 20 minutes. Stir once during baking.

Scripture Cake

3 C. I Kings 4:22	2½ C. Exodus 16:31
1 C. I Kings 4:22	5 Isaiah 10:14
1 tsp. Leviticus 2:13	2 C. Numbers 17:8
2 tsp. Solomon 4:16	2 C. I Samuel 30:12
1½ C. Judges 5:25	1 C. Isaiah 7:22 (melted)

Follow Solomon's advice from Proverbs 23:14 for making a better boy. Bake at 350° until done.

Date Fingers

¼ C. peanut oil	½ tsp. Royal baking powder
1½ C. honey	1 C. chopped dates
3 eggs, well beaten	1 C. chopped pecans
1 C. whole wheat flour	

Preheat oven to 350°. Line a square pan with wax paper, rub the paper with butter. Mix the ingredients together well and spread the mixture in the pan. Bake for 15 to 20 minutes, cool, and cut into rectangles. These may be rolled in coconut if cut when warm.

Zabaglione

6 egg yolks	⅛ tsp. salt
6 tbsp. brown sugar or honey	⅛ tsp. ground mace or nutmeg
¾ C. Marsala wine	

Arrange a double boiler so the water in the bottom part does not touch the top section. Combine all of the ingredients in the top section. Cook over simmering water, beating constantly with a portable beater until mixture is thick and light. It will swell to about 3 or 4 times its original volume. Avoid overcooking, or the mixture may curdle. From time to time, while beating, it may be necessary to scrape the sides of the pan with a spoon to prevent a thick layer from forming. Serve while warm in parfait glasses, glass punch cups, or any glass dessert dish. Zabaglione may also be served over cooked or canned fruit, like pears or peaches, or over light spongecake or ladyfingers. Serves 4. This recipe was given to Linda Weisburg by Olive Landers.

The Marshalls Sweet Potato Pudding

6 C. fresh mashed sweet
  potatoes
2 tsp. cinnamon
1 tsp. powdered mace
2 tsp. nutmeg

1½ C. shredded coconut
1 C. clover honey
6 eggs
½ C. peanut oil
2 C. non-fat milk

Mix all ingredients together and bake at 350° for about 40 minutes, in a greased pan.

Whole Wheat Pie Crust

2 C. whole wheat pastry flour
½ tsp. salt
½ C. wheat germ

¾ C. butter or margarine
½ C. ice water

Combine flour, salt, and wheat germ in a large bowl. Add butter and mix with a fork until mix looks like crumbled peas. Sprinkle in ice water and continue to mix. Don't over handle the crust. Roll out on a floured board. Use in your favorite pie recipe.

Unbleached Flour Pie Crust

2 C. unbleached white flour
¼ C. soy flour
½ tsp. salt

¾ C. butter or margarine
¾ C. ice water

Combine flours, salt, and butter or margarine, and mix with a fork, by hand or with a pastry cutter. Using the hands is quick and fun, too. When the mixture is well blended, add the ice water all at once and mix. Roll out on a slightly floured board and use in your favorite recipe for pies or pastry.

Concord Grape Pie

4 C. Concord grapes
1 C. honey
3 tbsp. tapioca

1 tbsp. lemon juice
Pastry for 2-crust pie
2 tbsp. butter

About 2 hours before baking or early in the day slip skins from grapes, reserving skins. In a medium saucepan over high heat, bring grape pulp to boiling, stirring occasionally. Reduce heat to low and simmer 5 minutes, stirring. Press the pulp through a sieve into a medium bowl to remove seeds. Add grape skins, honey, tapioca, and lemon juice; mix well. Let stand while preparing pastry. Preheat oven to 425°. Roll out half of the pastry and use it to line a pie plate. Fill with grape mixture; dot with butter. Prepare the top crust, making a decorative edge. Bake 25 minutes or until golden. Serve warm or cold.

Blackberry Pie

1 C. honey
¼ C. unbleached flour
½ tsp. cinnamon
½ tsp. grated lemon peel

¼ tsp. nutmeg
5 C. fresh blackberries
Pastry for 2-crust pie
1 tbsp. butter

About 2 hours before baking or early in the day combine the first 6 ingredients in a large bowl and let stand. Preheat oven to 425°. Roll out half of the pastry and line a pie plate. Spoon the filling evenly into the crust; dot with butter. Prepare the top crust, making a decorative edge. Bake 50 minutes or until golden.

Rhubarb Pie

1½ C. honey
¼ C. whole wheat flour
1 tbsp. grated orange peel

4 C. rhubarb, cut into 1" pieces
Pastry for 2-crust pie
2 tbsp. butter

About 1¼ hours before baking or early in the day combine honey, flour, orange peel, and salt. Add rhubarb and toss well. Let stand while preparing pastry. Preheat oven to 425°. Roll out half of the pastry and line the pie plate. Spoon filling evenly into the crust; dot with butter. Prepare the top crust. Bake 40 to 50 minutes, until the crust is golden. Serve.

Gooseberry Pie

4 C. gooseberries
2 C. honey
¼ C. arrowroot
½ tsp. cinnamon

¼ tsp. salt
Pastry for 2-crust pie
1 tbsp. butter

About 2 hours before baking or early in the day: If gooseberries are large, slice in half. In medium bowl combine honey, arrowroot, cinnamon, and salt; add gooseberries and toss well. With a slotted spoon, mash the berries so that all the honey mixture is moistened. Let stand while preparing pastry. Preheat oven to 400°. Roll out half of the pastry and line the pie plate. Spoon gooseberry filling evenly into the crust; dot with butter. Prepare the top crust. Bake 10 minutes; turn oven control to 325° and bake 1 hour more or until the pastry is golden. During the last 15 minutes or so of baking, place a sheet of foil just below the shelf with the pie to catch any drippings.

Sour Cream Pie

2 C. sour cream
4 eggs
2 C. seedless raisins
2 tsp. cinnamon
1 tsp. nutmeg

1 tsp. allspice
1 C. pitted & chopped dates
2 C. dark corn syrup
1 C. brown sugar
2 unbaked pie shells

Beat all ingredients together and pour in two unbaked pie shells. Bake at 350° for 35 minutes.

Summer Squash Pie

2 C. cooked mashed squash	¼ tsp. grated ginger
1 C. honey	2 C. non-fat milk
¼ tsp. powdered mace	2 tsp. vanilla
¼ tsp. cinnamon	4 eggs, beaten
¼ tsp. ground cloves	½ C. brown sugar
¼ tsp. nutmeg	2 unbaked pie shells

Beat all ingredients together. Pour in unbaked pie shells. Bake at 400° for 10 minutes, lower heat and bake at 325° for 30 minutes.

Apple Dumplings

1 recipe of unbleached pie crust	Juice of 1 lemon
10 apples, peeled and cored, left whole	1 lb. dark brown sugar
2 tbsp. cinnamon	¼ lb. butter, melted

Peel apples and place in cold water. Add lemon juice to keep the apples from turning dark. Combine brown sugar, cinnamon, and melted butter. Remove apples from water and dry off with a paper towel. Cut pie crust in 6" squares and place in a greased shallow pan. Set an apple in the center of each square, add 2 tablespoons of sugar mix, and fold up each corner of the dough. Continue until all apples are covered. Sprinkle remaining sugar mixture over all and bake at 325°, for 45 minutes, or until golden brown. Your guests and family will praise you over and over again.

Carob Ice Cream

1 C. carob powder	3 eggs, beaten
2 C. evaporated milk	4 C. heavy cream
2 C. honey	2 tbsp. vanilla extract or
½ tsp. salt	ground vanilla beans

Heat milk over boiling water. Add carob powder and beat with electric beater until well blended. Combine honey and salt. Mix well. Gradually add to the carob mixture and cook until thickened, stirring constantly. Continue to cook for 5 minutes more. Add eggs, stirring vigorously. Cook 2 minutes longer, stirring all the while. Cool. Add cream and vanilla. Pour into ice cream maker can and freeze, using 8 parts ice to 1 part salt.

Vanilla Ice Cream

1 C. honey	2 C. heavy cream
½ tsp. salt	1 tbsp. vanilla extract or
6 eggs yolks, beaten	ground vanilla beans
2 C. evaporated milk	

Mix honey, salt, and egg yolks thoroughly. Add the milk slowly and cook in the top of a double boiler until the mixture coats a spoon. Cool. Strain, and add cream and vanilla. Pour into ice cream maker can and freeze using 8 parts ice to 1 part salt.

Carrot Ice Cream

2 C. heavy cream	3 C. fresh carrot juice
1 C. honey	2 tsp. vanilla

Mix ingredients well and freeze in ice cream freezer. If you don't have an ice cream freezer, this method works just as well: Pour mixture in a metal mixing bowl; cover and place in freezer compartment of refrigerator until crystals form. Remove and beat well. Return to freezer until mushy but not quite solid. Remove and beat again. Place back in freezer until ready to serve.

Honey Nut Ice Cream

2 C. evaporated milk
2 C. heavy cream
½ tsp. salt
4 egg yolks, beaten

2 C. boiling water
1½ C. honey
1½ C. chopped pecans

Pour the milk into a freezing tray and freeze until ice crystals form around the edges of the tray. Add salt to the beaten egg yolks and add boiling water, stirring constantly. Cook over double boiler for 4 to 5 minutes. Cool, and add honey. Whip chilled cream until stiff. Fold into cold custard, adding nuts, and freeze until firm. Pour warm honey over and sprinkle with pecans.

Peach Ice Cream

1½ C. honey
½ tsp. salt
2 C. evaporated milk
3 eggs, beaten

1 C. fresh peaches, mashed
2 C. heavy cream
2 tsp. vanilla extract

Stir honey, salt and milk in the top of a double boiler. Heat. Add eggs and beat with an electric beater. Cook for 10 minutes. Cool. Add all the rest of the ingredients and beat for 2 minutes. Pour into ice cream maker can and freeze, 8 parts ice to 1 part salt.

Honey Ice Cream

4 eggs, separated
1 C. honey

4 C. cream
2 tsp. vanilla extract

Beat egg yolks until thick, adding honey slowly. Blend in cream and vanilla. Freeze until firm. Place in a chilled bowl. Add egg whites and beat until smooth. Return to freezing tray and freeze until firm.

Lemon Ice Cream

1 tbsp. unbleached flour	2 eggs, slightly beaten
1½ C. honey	3 C. evaporated milk
½ tsp. salt	½ C. strained lemon juice
1 C. boiling water	2 tbsp. grated lemon rind

Blend flour, honey, and salt in the top of a double boiler. Add boiling water and heat to boiling over direct heat, stirring frequently. Pour slowly over eggs. Return to the double boiler and cook 5 minutes, stirring constantly. Remove from heat. Cool. Add milk, lemon juice, and rind. Pour into ice cream maker can and freeze, using 8 parts ice to 1 part salt.

Fresh Strawberry Ice Cream

2 eggs, beaten well	1 C. evaporated milk
1 C. honey	1 tsp. vanilla extract
½ tsp. salt	2 C. heavy cream
1 C. mashed strawberries	

Combine ingredients and beat well. Pour into freezer can and freeze, using 8 parts ice to 1 part salt.

Wheat Germ Cookies

¼ lb. butter	½ C. sour cream
1 C. brown sugar	3 C. wheat germ
½ C. raw sugar	1 tsp. soda
1 egg	2 tsp. cloves

Cream together sugars and butter. Add egg and sour cream to sugar mixture. Stir dry ingredients together. Blend wet and dry ingredients together. Drop cookies on a greased cookie sheet, and flatten slightly. Bake until golden, about 12 to 15 minutes at 350°.

Nut Cookies

1 stick butter, softened	2 C. whole wheat pastry flour
2 eggs, beaten	1 tsp. soda
1½ C. honey	½ tsp. salt
1 C. chopped nuts	

Beat eggs and butter together, add honey and beat. Add flour, salt, soda, and nuts, and beat wet ingredients. I use pecans or peanuts for the nuts. Roll in balls, and place on greased cookie sheet 2-3 inches apart. Bake at 350°, about 15 minutes.

Coconut Cookies

2 eggs	1 tsp. salt
1 stick butter	1 tsp. soda
1½ C. honey	2 C. grated fresh coconut
1½ C. whole wheat pastry flour	½ C. raw sugar

Beat eggs and butter together, add honey and beat. Add flour, salt, soda, and coconut to wet ingredients. Drop by spoonfuls on greased cookie sheet. Flatten with bottom of a glass dipped in raw sugar. Bake at 375°, for 12 to 15 minutes.

Honey Cookies

1 stick butter	1 tsp. soda
1½ C. honey	1 tsp. nutmeg
1 egg, beaten	1 tsp. cinnamon
½ C. sour cream	1 tsp. cloves
5 C. whole wheat pastry flour	1 tsp. salt

Cream butter and honey together. Add eggs and sour cream to butter mixture, and beat until well blended. Stir dry ingredients together until well mixed. Add dry ingredients to wet ingredients a little at a time, until mixture is nice and creamy. These cookies may be formed with a pastry bag or dropped by spoonfuls on a greased cookie sheet. Bake about 15 minutes at 350°.

Raisin Treasure Cookies

1 stick butter
2 C. whole wheat pastry flour
½ tsp. salt
½ tsp. cinnamon
1 C. raw sugar
1 tsp. Royal baking powder

1 tsp. grated lemon rind
1 C. chopped pecans
1½ C. raisins
2 eggs, beaten
5 tbsp. milk

Cream butter. Stir flour, salt, cinnamon, sugar, and baking powder together. Blend butter and dry ingredients together until well blended. Add all remaining ingredients and mix thoroughly. Drop by spoonfuls onto a greased cookie sheet. Bake at 350°, about 15 minutes.

Nut Bars

1 C. whole wheat flour
1½ C. brown sugar
¾ stick butter
2 eggs, beaten

1 C. dark corn syrup
¼ stick butter, melted
2 tbsp. vanilla
1½ C. chopped English walnuts

Mix together well, flour, 1 C. brown sugar, ¾ stick butter. Press this mixture into medium square pan or medium biscuit pan. Bake 15 minutes at 350°. Remove from oven, and cover with a mixture of eggs, ½ C. brown sugar, corn syrup, melted butter, vanilla, and nuts. Bake 25 minutes more at 350°. Cool and cut into bars.

Carob Brownies

2 C. carob powder	3 eggs, beaten
½ C. corn oil	1 C. raw sugar
½ C. whole wheat flour	1 tsp. vanilla
¼ tsp. salt	½ C. honey
1 tsp. Royal baking powder	1½ C. pecans, halves or pieces

Combine carob powder and oil together and mix well. Stir flour, salt, and baking powder together. Cream eggs and sugar gradually, beating until light. Add vanilla and flour mix to carob mixture. Add honey and egg mixture, and nuts, and mix well. Spread in greased medium square or shallow biscuit pan. Bake 350° for 30 minutes. Cut in bars.

Granola Cookies

1½ sticks butter	1½ C. whole wheat flour
3 C. wheat germ	1 tsp. soda
1½ C. Granola	2 eggs, beaten
1½ C. honey	¼ C. milk

Cream butter; add honey. Stir wheat germ, granola, flour, and soda together. Blend butter mix and dry ingredients together until well blended. Add all remaining ingredients and mix thoroughly. For crisper cookies, omit or reduce the amount of flour. Roll in balls and place on greased cookie sheet 2 to 3 inches apart; they will spread out as they bake. Flatten with wet fingertips. Bake at 350°, about 10 to 12 minutes.

Caraway Treats

1 egg	2 C. unbleached white flour or
1 C. raw sugar	or whole wheat flour
Juice of 1 lemon	1 C. soy flour
1 stick butter	1 tsp. soda
2½ tsp. caraway seeds	½ tsp. salt

Beat egg, add sugar gradually, and continue beating. Add lemon juice, butter, and caraway seeds. Stir dry ingredients together and add to mixture, mixing well. Roll in parchment paper. Chill. Slice thinly and bake on greased cookie sheet at 400° for 10 minutes.

Sesame Candy I

1½ C. toasted sesame seeds	3 tbsp. carob powder
¾ C. grated fresh coconut	½ C. honey
¼ C. chopped pecans	2 tbsp. vanilla

Mix all ingredients together, reserving ½ C. seeds and ½ C. coconut. Form into balls. Roll in toasted sesame seeds, coat in coconut, and chill.

Sesame Candy II

2 C. raw sesame seeds	3 tbsp. peanut oil
1 C. honey	

Mix honey and sesame seeds together. Pour peanut oil in bottom of iron skillet. Pour sesame-honey mixture in skillet. Bake at 350° until bubbling. Cool at room temperature for 1 hour. Crack and remove from pan. Cover.

Appendix I:

A brief summary on Edgar Cayce for those of you who are unfamiliar with the work of this remarkable man. Edgar Cayce was born near Hopkinsville, Kentucky, on March 18, 1877 and died January 3, 1945. Throughout his 67 years he used his psychic ability unselfishly to help others. Edgar Cayce was deeply religious. It is said that he read the Bible at least once for every year of his life.

"Reading" is a term used to describe the clairvoyant discourse which Edgar Cayce gave while in a self-induced hypnotic sleep-state. The Edgar Cayce readings on health and diet are a great phenomenon—yet true. The accuracy of his readings in the "collective unconscious" state was not confined to the physical, but mental and emotional as well. By having only the name and the geographical location of an individual, he was able to give a detailed diagnosis of the physical condition.

Careful documentation of the readings and follow-up responses from people who were helped by Cayce's advice support the accuracy of his recommendations. Some of these treatments were regarded as unusual at the time, but have, over the years, proven their effectiveness. A diet high in fiber, low in saturated fats, and rich in natural vitamins has been stressed in recent years by a variety of nutritionists; Edgar Cayce was emphasizing such foods in the 1920s and 1930s. Cayce warned against over-refined and over-processed foods; today there is medical corroboration of the toxic effects of pesticides, artificial dyes, and synthetic additives.

Using suggestions from the Edgar Cayce readings on diet and health, the recipes in this book were developed to encourage individuals from all walks of life to eat better, so that they may live healthier and happier lives. The excerpts from the readings in this book pertain to the normal diet.

The Cayce readings in *The New Life Cookbook* can be employed in two ways. First, they can help the reader work out a total plan for personal nutrition, and second they can quickly answer simple everyday questions regarding food combinations and nutrition based on the Cayce readings.

Yes, it is true that much of the content of the physical readings applies only to certain individuals; there are, however, hundreds of readings that apply to all. It is from this group that I have chosen these readings and based the recipes in this book.

From reading 1183-2: Then the diet: This should not be so rigid as to appear that you can't do this or you can't do that, but rather let the attitudes be...everything that is eaten, as well as every activity ...purposeful in conception, constructive in nature. Analyze that: purposeful in activity, constructive in nature!

Correct balance is what we are looking for—80% alkaline to 20% acid-producing foods. Therefore, an abundance of vegetables and fruits will help to maintain alkalinity of the system. Lemons and lemon juice are very good alkalizers.

In 1931 The Association for Research and Enlightenment was founded and more information can be found on the Edgar Cayce readings at the A.R.E. headquarters in Virginia Beach, Virginia, where the trace readings are located and have been indexed and cross-indexed, providing research facilities and in-depth information on all of the readings that were recorded.

ALKALINE PRODUCING FOODS (80% of the diet)

Eggs (yolks only)

Fruits (all fresh and dried except cranberries, plums, and large prunes)

Milk (all forms)

Vegetables (all fresh and dehydrated, except legumes and rhubarb)

ACID PRODUCING FOODS (20% of the diet)

Animal fats
Beef
Brains
Bread
Chicken
Coconut
Corn meal
Dried beans
Dried peas
Duck
Egg (whites only)
Filberts
Goose
Grains
Hearts

Kidneys
Lamb
Lentils
Liver
Peanuts
Pecans
Pork
Rhubarb
Sweetbreads
Syrup
Turkey
Vegetable oils
Walnuts
White sugar
Wild game

710-1: Of course, do not diet self so that it becomes rote, or the necessity of refusing—or adhering in this or that direction; but we would keep a well-balance.

1523-3: Q-5. What foods are acid-forming for this body?
A-5. All of those that are combining fats with sugars. Starches naturally are inclined for acid reaction. But a normal diet is about twenty percent acid to eighty percent alkaline producing.

888-1: In the matter of the diet, be more mindful that there are less of the acid-producing foods; more of carbohydrates—that is, sweets— but sweets such as honey, fruits, nuts, wine; but only a small quantity of red wine each day, only with black or brown bread—this would make for a stimulating of the whole system.

1710-10: Q-6. Suggest foods to stress and foods to avoid in the diet.
A-6. Avoid those combinations that produce acidity in the system. Not that these suggestions should be used to such measures as to eliminate acids entirely, but that there be kept a normal balance. Avoid the combination of fats with butterfats, as with the white of an egg, or white bread, or rice, or those that produce that character of starch. Brown bread, corn bread and such are much preferable. All vegetables; and do have at least once each day some raw vegetables.

1695-2: Do take D and G, but these more in the foods than supplementing in the combinations. These will bring better forces to the body; that is, in the food values take sea foods, fowl, a little lamb; not other meats. Plenty of carrots, beets, onions, lettuce, celery.

1771-3: Use fruits, nuts, berries of all natures or characters that are grown in the environ of the body, especially.

811-7: Those that carry vitamins A and B and B-1 especially should be taken by the body. These are found most, of course, in the fruits and vegetables of the yellow variety, as well as especially in marrow, beef, *and* liver, tripe and the like.

1523-3: Q-10. Suggest diet beneficial to preserving teeth.

A-10. Eggs, potato peelings, sea foods—all of these are particularly given to preserving the teeth; or anything that carries quantities of calcium or aids to the thyroids in its production would be beneficial—so it is not overbalanced, see?

1151-2: Not white bread and potatoes at the same meal. Not quantities of sweets *with* white bread. The meats and sweets should be preferably taken at the same meal. It isn't so much *what* the body eats as it is the *combinations* that are taken at times. Beware then of those things. No *red* meats; that is, rare meats. In meats, preferably use fish, fowl or lamb, rather than other types. have three vegetables grown above the ground to one under the ground. Have one meal each day, if possible, with *only RAW* vegetables. Nuts are good, but do not combine same with meats. Let them take the place of same. Filberts and almonds are preferable in the nuts.

805-2: As potatoes, whether white or the yam activity with butter, should not be taken with fats or meats; but using these as a portion of one meal with *fruits* or vegetables is well. When meats are taken, use mutton, fowl or the like, and do not have heavy starches with same—but preferably fruits or vegetables. These will be found to be much more preferable. Fresh fruits, nuts, and the like, taken as a part of a meal at different periods, as the body finds that the system is able to handle same, are more preferable to combining so many in one period.

543-7: Noon—preferably green vegetables, with mayonnaise or dressings that are palatable to the body. There may also be taken at this period broths, or such, and *hard* breads—see? that make an activity especially in the glands which secrete for digestion.

4008-1: Do not take quantities of such as beans, dried or the dry or fresh beans where they are shelled—as butter beans or lima beans—with white bread.

1188-10: A growing body requires plenty of vitamins A and B and D and C, that the structural portions may also have sufficient from the assimilated foods, rather than being supplied from concentrated forms of same.

890-1: In the matter of the diet, well that this be that which would supply a sufficient quantity of those vitamins necessary for increased blood and nerve energies for the system; and should naturally be of the alkaline type. (That is, green vegetables, fruits and milk products.)

3747-1: The diets will be along those lines that make for nerve *building*. Plenty of the green foods—as celery, salsify—not too much of the asparagus, but only those of the fresh or the green—cabbage, lentils, peas, beans, and such—these may be taken. Little or no meats, to be sure—though those that will add for nerve forces, as tripe, brains, kidneys, liver, spleen, or such, these will be beneficial to the body in small quantities.

710-1: . . . and fats. No fried meats. Beware of fried potatoes. Beware of *any* fried vegetables or cakes with syrup or any large quantities of the sweetmeats or very rich foods where too much of the nuts of certain natures are used: though nuts such as almonds, peanuts, English walnuts, Brazilian nuts and filberts are very good.

1586-1: Do not eat fried foods of any kind *ever;* especially not fried eggs, nor cakes—though buckwheat cakes may be taken if they are fried in butter and then *not* any butter used on same, but these should not be eaten with syrup. Honey—a little may be taken if so desired.

1852-1: Refrain altogether from fried foods, as much as practical.

1288-1: Do *not* combine ever any red meats with the starches, as of white bread or white potatoes, at the same meal. The meats should consist principally of fowl, fish or lamb. Not *any* fried foods at any time.

1586-1: Evenings—do not take fried foods morning, noon *or* evening! especially not fried potatoes, nor fried ham, nor fried meats—even fried chicken! But the meats—if any are taken should be preferably fish, fowl, or lamb; and these boiled, broiled or baked.

1703-1: Rather use lamb or fowl, broiled, roasted or the like—but *not* fried!

1337-1: Do not have any fried foods, especially as of steak or things of that nature—but broiled, boiled or the like; and especially fish, fowl or lamb should be used if meats at all are taken.

675-1: Fish may be taken occasionally; preferably that which is *not* fried but boiled, broiled or the like. Fowl and mutton may be taken. Do not have fried food, such as steak or very fat roasts—they are detrimental to the better eliminations from the system.

4874-3: A-7. Follow the suggestions as have been given, and that which assimilates and agrees with the system—but do *not* use hog meat in any character or manner!

2947-1: No hog meat of *any* character. Let there be plenty of fish and fowl, occasionally lamb.

2977-1: Fish, fowl and lamb are preferable to other foods as meats. Never hog meat, save crisp breakfast bacon.

4008-1: Fish, fowl and lamb are preferable as meats.

2679-1: Then, have especially those foods that carry more of the calcium and of the vitamins A, D, B-1 and other B complexes. Hence we would have plenty of fish, fowl, lamb and liver; these alternated as parts of the diet.

2084-15: Fish should be taken occasionally, sea foods especially.

2947-1: Keep the diets body-building. Plenty of vitamins A and D; plenty of B-1 and the B-Complex; or plenty of fish....

5394-1: Do take a great deal of fowl—as bird, chicken or the like, see? this well cooked but never fried. Do chew the bones, especially the bony pieces. These are much preferable to the breast or the like; the feet, wings, legs, ends of the bone should be chewed thoroughly, as it is from these that we may obtain the elements needed.

2084-15: When fowl is taken choose rather the very small bony pieces rather than what might appear to be the more delicate. Take those that are not supposed to be choice pieces—as the wimblebit, the back, the neck, the feet. All of these are much preferable and have much more vital energies for body building.

5672-1: Evenings—particularly blood building foods, as of liver or tripe, or of pig knuckle, or of blood pudding.

418-2 Noons—beef juices or broths, but do not take the broths of beef and beef juice—for they don't work very well together.

257-7: . . . taking those properties as the diet that give the rebuilding for the blood supply of system, as we would find in meat broths, beef or mutton, and of quantities of celery and of all green vegetable forces that will digest with the system, and relieve strain from the nerve supply, that with the assimilation of same gives that vital force necessary for the rebuilding in nerve supply through each plexus.

5394-1: In building up the body with foods, preferably have a great deal of raw vegetables for this body—as lettuce, celery, carrots, watercress. All we would take raw, with dressing, and oft with gelatin. These should be grated, or cut very fine, or even ground, but do preserve all of the juices with them when these are prepared in this manner in the gelatin.

4033-1: Vegetables that are raw, especially such as watercress, celery, lettuce, carrots should be prepared often—in fact, have some of these every day, but prepare most often with gelatin because of the activities that cause the better nerve forces.

3326-1: Watercress, especially, should be taken—and these raw; including celery and lettuce; at times carrots. All of these grated and combined with the gelatin would be much better for the body.

3429-1: In the diet keep plenty of raw vegetables, such as watercress, celery, lettuce, tomatoes, carrots, Change these in their manner of preparation, but do have some of these each day. They may be prepared rather often with gelatin, as with lime or lemon gelatin—or Jello. These will not only taste good but be good for you.

849-75: Q-4. Please explain the vitamin content of gelatin. There is no reference to vitamin content on the package.

    A-4. It isn't the vitamin content but it is ability to work with the activities of the glands, causing the glands to take from that absorbed or digested the vitamins that would not be active if there is not sufficient gelatin in the body. See, there may be mixed with any chemical that which makes the rest of the system susceptible or able to call from the system that needed. It becomes then, as it were, "sensitive" to conditions. Without it there is not that sensitivity.

935-1: Preferably use the *oil* dressings; as olive oil with paprika, or such combinations. even egg may be included in same, preferably the hard egg (that is the yolk) and it worked into the oil as a portion of the dressing.

1225-1: Noon—We would give those that carry more of the silicon, lime, salts—*these*, as we find, will be in the *green* vegetables. These in the form of salads, with any of the dressings that may make the salad the more palatable, including in these plenty of celery—and *all* of the green vegetables....

1586-1: These may be combined in many varied ways: Celery, lettuce, tomatoes, radish, peppers, cabbage, spinach, mustard, leeks, onions. Any or all of these may be combined.

846-1: In the middle of the day, or at least *one* meal a day—whether in the middle of the day or in the evening—should consist almost entirely of raw fresh vegetables; as tomatoes, celery, lettuce, carrots, spinach, onions, radishes and the like. These are more preferable to be taken with an oil or salad dressing.

4008-1: Have at least once every day a raw vegetable salad; such as watercress, celery, lettuce, raw carrots, onions, radishes or the like, with other foods.

977-1: Do take artichokes in *all* their forms, for this will aid in keeping a better balance in those tendencies for disturbances of circulation between the pancreas and the liver, as well as the kidneys. These should be taken raw at times, and cooked at times, when the Jerusalem artichoke is taken. Vary these. When the French or the bulb character artichoke is used, have plenty of butter with same. But these are good for the body.

2947-1: Beets and beet tops should be included in the diet; radishes, and the yellow yams should be included.

584-5: Quite a dissertation might be given as to the effect of tomatoes upon the human system. Of all the vegetables, tomatoes carry most of the vitamins in a well-balanced assimilative manner for the activities in the system. Yet if these are not cared for properly, they may become very destructive to a physical organism; that is, if they ripen after being pulled, or if there is the contamination with other influences. . . .

The tomato is one vegetable that in most instances (because of the greater uniform activity) is preferable to be eaten after being canned, for it is then much more uniform.

Q-3. What brand of canned tomatoes is best?

A-3. Libby's are more *uniform* than most.

2309-1: As to the diet—take plenty of food values that carry vitamin B-1 and G. These are found especially in carrots (cooked or raw—and we would have them both ways often), the yellow neck squash, yellow peaches, cereals—especially oats and corn.

1337-1: Do not have white potatoes, spaghetti, macaroni or corn—and two of these at the same meal.

846-1: *Do not* have cereals at the same meal with citrus fruits or citrus fruit juices; though they may be taken an hour or more apart, for their combination with the gastric juices of the stomach produces rather an acid than an alkaline.

710-1: But oranges, grapefruit, limes, lemons all may be taken, provided they are not taken close with any food that carries *gluten*— which would tend to change these in their activity with the gastric flows of the digestive areas.

418-2: *Do not* take citrus fruit juices *and* cereals at the same meal! Whole wheat toast, coddled eggs, little bacon, any or all of these may be taken; or stewed fruits, or baked apple, or the like. Any of these may be taken for the morning meal.

2072-2: Never combine fruit juices and cereals, however, at the same meal.

843-1: But do not take cereals with citrus fruit juices, or these at the same meals.

1484-1: Q-3. Are oranges considered the citrus fruit?

A-3. Oranges, pineapple, grapefruit, *all* may be taken. These are *not* acid-*producing.* They are alkaline reacting!

But when cereals or starches are taken, do not have the citrus fruit at the same meal—or even the same day; for such a combination in the system at the same time becomes *acid*-producing! Hence those taken on different days are well for the body.

1188-10: It is well for this body, or growing bodies, or elderlly individuals also, for strength building and for correcting the eliminations, to use this as a cereal, or a small quantity of this with the cereal, or it may be served with milk or cream:

Secure the unpitted Syrian or black figs and the Syrian dates. Cut or grind very fine a cup of each. Put them on in a double boiler with just a little goat's milk in same—a tablespoonful. Let come almost to a boil. Stir in a tablespoonful of yellow corn meal.

275-45: But for this particular body, equal portions of black figs or Assyrian figs and Assyrian dates—these ground together or cut very fine, and to a pint of such a combination put half a handful of corn meal, or crushed wheat. These cooked together—well, it's food for such a spiritually developed body as this!

1724-1: And whenever there is a great anxiety or stress, do not eat especially apples raw nor bananas nor fruits of that nature which are acid-producing, but rather use the easily assimilated foods.

935-1: Apples should only be eaten when cooked; preferably roasted and with butter or hard sauce on same, with cinnamon and spice.

509-2: Beware of apples, unless of the jenneting variety, but pears, bananas, oranges, grapefruit, plums, peaches, all of these may be taken in moderation and *in their season*. And use fruits that are *not* artificially ripened, even though it is necessary to use those that are canned; pineapple and pineapple juices are excellent for the body.

4841-1: For this condition of this body, we take that into the system which produces blood of a character that would act on to these forces where they are needed, or those of fruits, especially apples and pears, which contain or an iron condition which is in that, which we need into the blood or what produces blood of what we have not most in it in itself.

501-4: Q-6. Do avocado pears contain much iron and copper, and are they good for anemia?

A-6. They are good for anemia. They contain most iron. Pears are helpful to *anyone*, especially where body and blood building influences are needed; for they will be absorbed. These are best to be taken morning and evening; not through the active portions of the day.

3326-1: It would be well to include prunes in the diet, if they are cooked—or even fresh. Plums of all natures, then, are very well to be taken.

275-45: Q-7. What kind of fruit juice is best upon rising?

A-7. When orange juice is taken, always take a little lemon juice with same. Change these, but not too many combinations. Lime may be used with a little of the grapefruit, or the pineapple. Any of these are well, and the changing occasionally is preferable.

849-23: Watch the diets. Keep to those things that will aid in the eliminations. Build up the body with more of iron, as may be had from dried fruits, figs, dates, nuts and the like. Let these form a part of the daily diet, with plenty of oranges, lemons, grapefruit and especially *fresh* pineapple—rather than the canned, for this particular body. The green vegetables; these well-balanced, well-cooked.

2529-1: All of those fruits and vegetables, then, that are yellow in color should be taken; oranges, lemons, grapefruit, yellow squash, yellow corn, yellow peaches—all of these and such as these; beets—but all of the vegetables cooked in their *own* juices, and the body eating the juices with same.

1484-1: Noons—vegetable soups, or vegetables that are preferably of the leafy variety; or those that are of the bulbous nature, but these should be thoroughly cooked and *only* in their *own* juices (as in Patapar Paper)

1852-1: Q-6. Is it all right to use club aluminum waterless cooker for preparing my food?

A-6. This is very well, but *preferably* Patapar Paper is the better manner for preparing food, especially for this body during the periods that the properties or foods and the medicinal applications are being administered.

Of course, there are some foods that are affected in their activity by aluminum—especially in the preparation of certain fruits, or tomatoes, or cabbage. But most others, it is very well.

1196-7: Certain characters of food cooked in aluminum are bad for *any* system, and where a systemic condition exists—or a disturbed hepatic circulation of assimilating force—a disturbed hepatic eliminating force—they are naturally so. Cook rather in granite, or better still in Patapar Paper.

632-6: Use citrus fruits; all of these may be taken, as also may grapes, pears, pineapples or such natures. Preferably use the fresh fruits, or the nearer fresh fruits; preferably *none* that are canned with any preservative such as benzoate of soda! Use all the other vegtables that are well balanced.

543-7: Other fruits—such as the citrus fruits, grapes, pears, peaches (whether canned or otherwise, but if canned be sure they are *not* canned with benzoate of soda).

826-14: Green beans, not dried beans; lettuce, carrots—these cooked in their *own* juices and not just in water, but in Patapar Paper and the juices preserved in same. The fruits *and* the vegetables, not those that have been frozen but those that are preserved either in their own syrup or in the regular can syrup and *not* those prepared with benzoate or any preservative—for the benzoate becomes hard upon the system.

5672-1: *Do not* mix cereals and fruit juices, though cereals with fresh fruits may be taken—as sliced peaches, pears, or the like. Those that are canned may be taken, provided they are not canned—or preserved—with the benzoate of soda.

1484-1: As for drinks, none of those that are made with carbonated waters. Those that are of the pure nature are preferable.

2157-2: Q-3. Are soft drinks all right for this body?
A-3. No; for very few bodies, and not for this body either!

1225-1: Not too much of pastries that carry the cane sugars, but those that make for lime, silicon, magnesia—these will be well.

1188-10: Not too much of sugars, yet sufficient. Let the sweets be taken in such forms as of honey, fruits, corn or Karo syrup. These are body-building; also supply energies that are well for a growing developing body.

2157-2: If taking sweets, use either Karo or honey.

808-3: Q-13. What type of sweets may be eaten by the body?
A-13. Honey, especially in the honeycomb; or preserves made with *beet* rather than cane sugar. Not too great a quantity of these, of course, but the forces in sweets to make for the proper activity through the action of the gastric flows *are* as necessary as body-building; for these become body-building in making for the proper fermentation (if it may be called so) in the digestive activities. Hence two or three times a week the honey upon the bread or the food values would furnish that necessary in the whole system.

2309-1: Whole wheat bread always, and preferably this toasted.

821-1: Preferably use the whole wheat or whole meal to the white flour or white bread.

675-1: Do not use white bread at any time, but only the whole wheat or rye bread—and this preferably toasted.

1484-1: Only use brown bread, or preferably for this body, as much as possible only Ry-Krisp.

1703-1: Mornings—citrus fruit juices, in their combinations, *or* cereals. When cooked cereal is used, preferably use only the whole wheat. This may be merely rolled, crushed or ground—but the *whole* of the grain is to be taken; because of the influence and vitamins, as well as the iron, as well as the very natures of the life of the wheat itself that are needed. Crushed or ground, then—whole.

556-8: . . . . whole wheat that is rolled and then cooked for two or two and a half hours—only, though, in enamel or glassware. While this carries a great deal of starch, it would be very strengthening and helpful if taken in moderation . . . .

5672-1: . . . cooked cereals, preferably of Wheatena or rolled oats, but the oats should be the steel cut oats rather than those already heated, for they lose some of the necessary vitamins in such. Those that are cooked for a long period of time.

2679-1: Use plenty of whole wheat grain—as cracked wheat, crushed or steel cut oats, and plenty of citrus fruits. However, *do not* use citrus fruits *and* cereals at the same meal. Rather alternate these, having one on one day, the other the next, and so on.

2977-1: Corn cakes, corn bread would be good; provided sweets are not eaten with same.

2072-2: Fruits and nuts in their season should be taken, especially almonds and filberts.

3180-3: An almond a day is much more in accord with keeping the doctor away, especially certain types of doctors, than apples. For the apple was the fall, not almond—for the almond blossomed when everything else died. Remember this is life!

1409-9: Butter fats and cheeses and such are well to be taken in moderation.

1703-2: Q-15. And milk, I find, makes more mucus, the basis for catarrh.

A-15. This if taken properly is *not* the basis of mucus. If this is thy experience, then there are other conditions producing same. For milk, whether it is the dry or the pasteurized or raw, is near to the perfect combination of forces for the human consumption.

846-1: Yogurt and such combinations, which arise as the basis for cheese, is very good; especially for the colon condition.

567-8: A-3. Egg white, unless it is prepared in the form of a coddled egg, makes for a formation of acid by the extra amount of those qualities that we find in same. With the changes that are wrought, it would be very good to use the whole egg—provided it is coddled or soft-scrambled.

826-14: Use not the vegetable oils in the cooking, but either the peanut oil or the Parkay margarine—for this especially carries D in a manner that conforms with these properties in preparation for assimilation by the body.

1620-3: As we find, the use of the iodized salt or kelp—as a sea salt— would be beneficial in the general meal. . . .

1586-1: And preferably use the sea salt entirely, or iodized salt—this is preferable.

Appendix II:

MENUS

MEAL PLANNING

Proper nutrition cannot happen unless all essential nutrients are taken; that is, carbohydrates, fats, protein, vitamins, minerals, and water are supplied and utilized in adequate balance to maintain health and mental well-being. No single substance will maintain vibrant health.

These menus are so well balanced that they do not have to be utilized in the order given. For example, if you would like Monday's breakfast with Wednesday's lunch or dinner, go right ahead. The proper balance is still there. By re-arranging meals, you can form a month of menus from the suggestions provided here. If you wish, turn to the list of acid-alkaline forming foods and plan your own, remembering the most important but simple rule of 20 percent acid to 80 percent alkaline forming foods.

BREAKFAST

MONDAY
Fresh Yogurt with Fresh Blueberries
Shirred Eggs with Cheese
Whole Wheat Toast
Orange Juice with a little Lemon Juice
Herb Tea or Sanka

TUESDAY
Fresh Yogurt
Granola with Dried Fruit
Non-fat Milk
Pineapple Juice with a little Lime Juice
Herb Tea or Sanka

WEDNEDSAY
Fresh Yogurt with Fresh Strawberries
Hot Buckwheat Pancakes with Honey or
Natural Maple Syrup
Baked Apples
Crisp Bacon Slices
Herb Tea or Sanka

THURSDAY
Fresh Yogurt
Spinach or Cheese Omelet
Bran Muffins with Honey
Herb Tea or Sanka

FRIDAY
Fresh Yogurt
Poached Eggs on Whole Wheat English Muffins
Crisp Bacon Slices
Stewed Prunes or Figs
Herb Tea or Sanka

SATURDAY
Fresh Yogurt
Oatmeal made with Steel-cut Oats
Non-fat Milk with Honey
Orange Juice with a little Lemon Juice
Herb Tea or Sanka

SUNDAY BRUNCH
Fresh Yogurt
Scrambled Eggs or Wheat Germ Pancakes
Crisp Bacon Slices
Scripture Bread with Whipped Butter and Honey
Juice
Herb Tea, Sanka or Milk

LUNCHEON

MONDAY
Egg Foo Young
Brown Rice
Sautéd Chinese Vegetables
Ginger Bread
Orange Peel Tea

TUESDAY
Lentil Soup II
Dandelion Salad with Garlic Dressing
Summer Squash Pie
Whole Wheat Bread
Peach Ice Cream
Herb Tea

WEDNESDAY
Cream of Salmon Soup
Crisp Spinach with Cottage Cheese Dressing
Golden Broiled Chicken
Baked Carrots
Sautéd Zucchini
Soybean Bread
Carob Cake
Herb Tea or Sanka

THURSDAY
Black Bean Soup
Raw Broccoli Salad with Oil and Vinegar Dressing with Herbs
Soybean Loaf I
Baked Turnips
Stewed Tomatoes
Peanut Bread
Date Fingers or Zabaglione
Herb Tea or Sanka

FRIDAY
Carrot Soup
Avocado Salad with Avocado Dressing
Lamb Casserole
Baked Beets
Apricot Nut Bread
Honey Nut Ice Cream
Herb Tea or Sanka

SATURDAY
Purée of Turnip Soup
Cranberry-Orange Molded Salad
Roast Turkey
Asparagus Spears
Lemon Bread
Apple Dumplings
Herb Tea or Sanka

SUNDAY
Lettuce Soup
Shrimp Louis with Louis Sauce
Bulgur Pilaf
Baked Big Blue

Onion Bread
Baked Brown Rice Custard
Herb Tea or Sanka

DINNER

MONDAY
Tomato Juice
Broiled Salmon Steaks
Sautéd Cabbage
Lima Bean Casserole
Whole Wheat Bread
The Marshalls Sweet Potato Pudding

TUESDAY
Chestnut Soup
Cucumber Mousse
Roast Goose
Cauliflower
Corn on the Cob
Applesauce Bread
Sour Cream Ginger Bread

WEDNESDAY
Vegetable Cream Soup
Chicory Crown Salad with Blue Cheese Dressing
Soybean Patties
Scripture Bread
Strawberry Natural Ice Cream

THURSDAY
Artichoke Soup
Peaches and Cream Salad
Creole Fillets
Baked Brown Rice or Bulgur
Brussels Sprouts
Chopped Fresh Spinach
Poppy Seed Bread or Whole Wheat Bread
Scripture Cake

FRIDAY
Onion Soup
Roast Turkey with Herb Dressing
Stewed Tomatoes
Fresh Collard Greens or Summer Squash
Rice Muffins
Blackberry Pie

SATURDAY
Potato Peel Soup Marshalls Style
Cucumber-Yogurt Salad
Chicken or Veal Mousse
Fresh Vegetables
Whole Wheat Bread
Granola Cookies

SUNDAY BUFFET
Stuffed Prunes and Dates
Fresh Fruit Kabob I
Cucumber Twist
Celery Curls
Vegetable Cutouts
Gelatin Balls

Toasted Almonds
Soybean Bits
Cauliflowerets
Fresh Mixed Greens

Include any cold meats or fish left over from previous days, sliced. Toast any bread that is left over. Serve any leftover desserts, cut in small neat pieces. Herb Tea or Sanka. Little preparation is needed for this lavish buffet that is both luscious and delectable.

Index